MW01530731

To:
Lucy, Tom & Tara —
Hope to see you
soon.
All the Best —
Jul 18. 99.

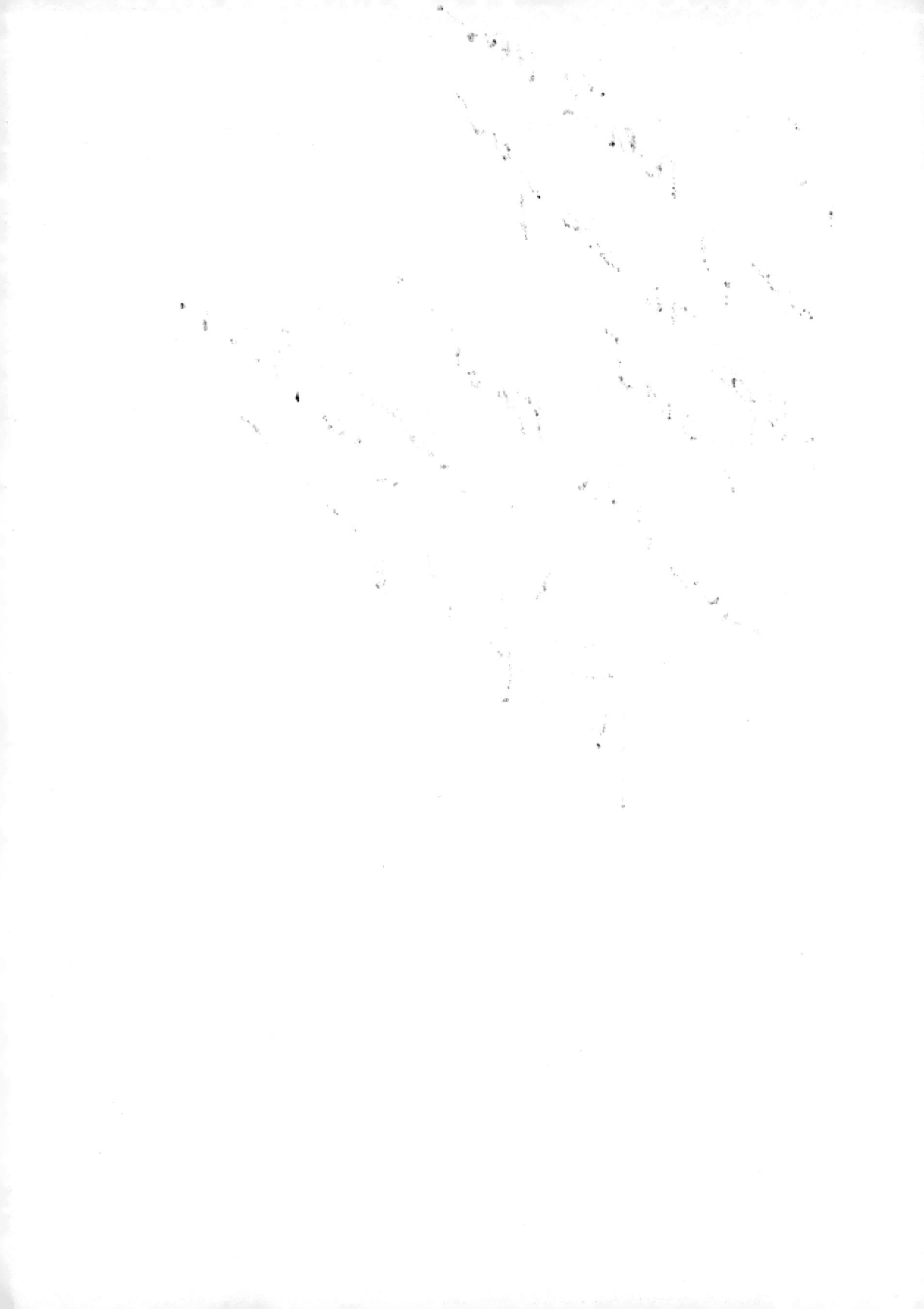

FROM THE ALAN BUNT JOURNAL

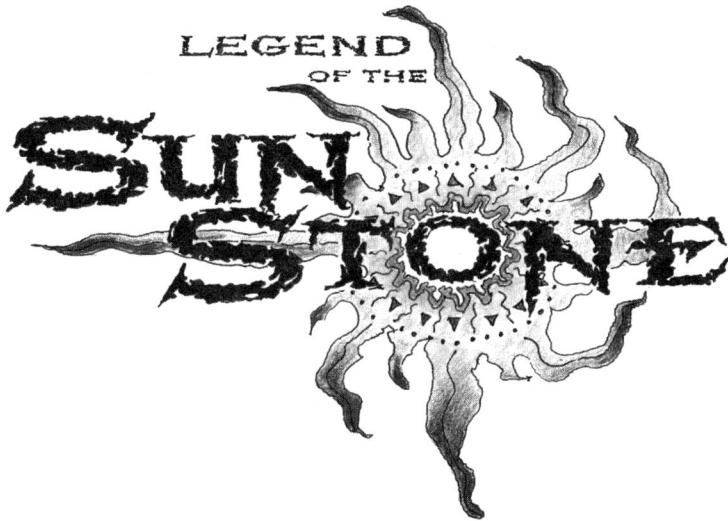

LEGEND OF THE SUN STONE

IN SEARCH OF THE LOST CITY

by
Eduardo A. Robles
and
Blanca Rosa A. Robles de Nuñez

Illustrations by:
Thanu Boonyawatana

Legend of the Sun Stone in Search of the Lost City

Published by:
Sun King Publishing
611 West Sixth Street, Suite 2880
Los Angeles, CA 90017
E-mail: sunkingpbl@earthlink.net

Library of Congress Catalog Card Number: 98-94026

ISBN: 0-9661738-0-5

Printed in the United States of America @
INSYNC.MEDIA
550 North Oak Street
Inglewood, California 90302
Cover designed by Judy Walker
Logo designed by Marc Romero
Editor Carolyn Porter

BELIEVE

Know this my Lord:

"That once a Kingdom flourished in the land where
God's Hand touched the earth. Where man lived in peace
with the animals, and magic lived in all things.
It is said the Kingdom was destroyed,
but I know it still exists.
For I have seen it, and once I lived there.
It cannot die, it never will.
But it is lost to those who do not believe.
Find the Sun Stone I tell you.
Find the Sun Stone and you will discover
the Kingdom of the Lost City in the Valley of the Sun."

Letter to the First Sun King written by Mur, Historian
and Magician 1014 A.D.

TABLE OF CONTENTS

THE LEOPARD MAN

PROLOGUE

1856

A spear slashed past his ear and lodged four inches into the baobab tree to his left. Barely glancing at the quivering shaft, he kept on running. The man was tall and strong, but his chest heaved as he ran, because of the weight of his leopard skin robes and what was slung across his chest. Still, he darted in and out of the foliage, constantly changing direction to avoid the deadly barbs of his enemy's weapons.

A huge leopard, appearing to guard the man's flank, emitted ferocious roars and pawed at the air with razor-sharp claws in the attempt to deter the army of pursuers. His threatening gestures did little to impede their progress. The assailants continued hot in pursuit, pausing only to reset an arrow or pull an errant spear from its lodging. The leopard spun away from the attackers, leaped over the undergrowth and raced after his master.

The leopard man never looked back. The thwack of arrows slamming nearby tree trunks or whistling past him as he fled let him know his pursuers were closing fast. He pulled his elegant robes around him tightly to protect his valuable package. He heard the thunder of crashing water in the distance and swiftly veered toward the sound. The roars of his mighty leopard guardian seem to spur him on.

Suddenly, a gruesome howl pierced the air. The sleek leopard pawed at the arrow that had found its mark in his side. His instinctual thrashing caused the shaft to break off, leaving four or five inches of the shaft exposed. Trembling, the leopard tried to get to his feet, only to fall on his side, causing the remaining piece of arrow to fully penetrate him. Even as darkness encompassed him, he lashed out furiously at the air around him in his last attempts to protect the leopard man.

Only minutes passed before three of the dogged pursuers cautiously approached the wounded animal, by now lying quietly on his side, gasping for breath. One muscular fellow, covered from head to toe in extraordinary bright paint, stepped forward. He hefted his spear and with a cry of victory, plunged it into the defenseless leopard. At that moment, the earth rumbled and shook violently.

Startled and frightened the men looked around them to see the trees swaying rapidly, some cracking and falling around them. Birds clamored shrilly, flapping their wings skyward. Monkeys chattered and screamed, falling from the shaking trees and running as fast as they could. Confusion momentarily halted the chase.

The leopard man stopped to let the earthquake have its say, thankful for the chance to catch his breath, but now he knew he was alone. As the quaking slowly subsided, he quickly pressed on. Weary, he reached the base of a waterfall, to the edge of the pool in which the tormented waters from above found solace. He climbed up the huge boulder looming east of the great falls, searching frantically for the path leading up to a cave hidden by the waterfall.

Several arrows glanced off of the cliff face above him. Obviously, his pursuers had recovered. He turned to survey the scene, determining the odds. As he wheeled about, an arrow tore into the outside of his left arm, the arrow's head exiting out the top of his biceps. The man broke the shaft of the arrow and pulled it out of his arm. With no perceivable hesitation, he began to climb, quickly following the narrow trail. The stark, red rocks served as cover from the pointed onslaught, and he made his way, unceasingly, to the lip of the cave. Not far behind, his pursuers had also found the trail. The man tried to shower them with a few rocks, but his injured arm and the need to protect his cargo prevented any adequate defense.

He plunged into the cave, feeling his way along the rough sides until his eyes adjusted to the darkness. He could hear, faintly, that his enemies would soon reach the mouth of the cave. Time was short.

He stumbled as he reached the end of the tunnel. Automatically protecting what he had carried so far, he thrust out his left arm to break the fall. He groaned in pain as the injured arm cushioned the blow of the hard rock. The noise of his assailants grew louder, closer.

Before him lay a span of rock that connected the cave mouth with a spiraling monolith that rose from the floor of a magnificent cavern. Light flooded the huge space, even though there were no openings in the ceiling to allow in sunlight. The man could see his way clearly to cross over the stone bridge. Struggling to his feet, he carefully put one foot in front of the other, making his way steadily, but slowly. He kept his eyes on his goal, not looking down, fearful that he would tumble the 39 meters below, perhaps goring himself on one of the golden stalactites that thrust up from the cavern floor. The noise of his pursuers echoed throughout the cavern.

Desperate, the man increased his pace across the bridge. Finally, he stepped onto the top of the monument, just as the first of his attackers appeared at the other side of the bridge.

The pursuer, with one strong motion, hurled his spear at the man. It found its mark. The spearhead dug deep into the leg of its target. But without hesitation, the man pulled the spear free and painfully limped to the altar in the middle of the monolith. He looked down at his leg and found it bleeding profusely. Tearing off a strip of his leopard-skin robe, he tied it tightly around his wound, slowing the flow of blood. He grimaced in pain, but there was not time for self-pity. The man looked up to see his pursuers carefully inching their way across the bridge.

Quickly, the man felt around his waistband, and finally pulled a bright glowing crystal from a pouch wrapped around the sling in which he carried his treasure. Raising the crystal in both hands above his head, he mumbled a few words, then plunged it into a hole in the altar, pushing it deep, securing its placement.

Abruptly, howling winds began to swirl about the cavern. His attackers stopped to brace themselves mid-bridge. A few were too late, and the winds blew them off of the bridge to smash onto the rocks below. The bridge began to crumble, and the man's attackers turned to flee back to the cave's mouth. Each scream of doom ended as a man hit the floor. Only two, by the man's count, made it back to the cave's mouth.

Swiftly turning, he limped to the top of the staircase that spiraled up and around the monolith from the cavern floor. He determinedly hobbled down the steps and found his was to the mouth of another tunnel to the east of the main cavern.

Blinded by the sun, he finally emerged from the end of the tunnel that overlooked a vast expanse, another world. He took coordinates from the sun, squared his shoulders, secured his burden and set his course southeast.

Tattered and covered with blood, he stumbled into the coastal town of Baratu. Oblivious to the stares of people on the street, he unerringly made his painful way to the waterfront, guided by the breathy hoot of the steam-whistle of a massive, twelve sail frigate preparing to lift anchor.

He looked toward the gangplank to see a group of women preparing to board. They began to ascend and reaching the deck, each turned to wave farewell to one of the gentlemen standing on the dock.

The man dragged himself toward the ship, pushing his way through the group of gentlemen. At last he reached the gangplank as the last woman stepped to board the ship. He managed to shout to her, "Help me. You must help me."

The astonished young woman turned toward his voice. Painfully, the man removed the sling from his shoulders. The first mate alerted the crew to the man's presence and those standing nearby began to close in on him. Barely able to speak, he held the bundle out to the woman, "Please. Be blessed. Take and guard with your life."

The woman, startled, began to speak, to protest. She faltered when she looked into the man's eyes. Then, as if in a trance, she held out her arms and received the bundle from him.

By this time a pool of blood had formed at the man's feet. As life began to desert him, he reeled and fell backwards. Staggering to maintain his balance, he tried to grab the rail. He missed, crushing his head on the dock as he plunged into the water below.

Suddenly, the horror of the man's demise was quickly forgotten as the cry of a baby escaped from the precious bundle the woman was left holding.

Montagnes ou il y a des Mines d'Argent: ez Bergen Zilver nen.

ROYᴹᵉ DE [KONINGʳ] SACOMBE

LES [DE] ZIMBAS

Cafres, amis des Portugais: KAFFERS, Vrienden der Portugeezen. Cuama

Fortᵉ de Maenbe Montagnᵉˢ dans le Lac de Rufombo: Bron van Maenbe, Berg in 't Meir.

Fort des Zimbas: Fort der Zimbas.

RO

ractes: Waterval len ova

R. Sabie.

Tete, Chateau bati par les Portugais: KASTEEL van de Portugeezen gebowd.

Montagne de Chiri très peuplé: Gebergte Chiri zeer Bevolkt.

ROYᵉ DE [KONINGʳ] MONGAS.

Jnaparapola Montᵉ Aiar ou il y a des Mines d'Or Abondantes Berg Alaar, daar Overvloed van Goud mynen zyn.

Mossapa.

Sena, ou Sᵗ Marsali

Cafres, alliés des Portugaˢ KAFFERS, Bondgenooten der Portugeezen

Mines d'Or: Goudmynen.

Inhamior, Capitale. Hoofstad.

Boror Roy

Mines d'Or: udmynen.

Montagne de Lupata Gebergte Lupata.

Luane

Rᵉ D'[KONINGʳ] INHAMIOR, dependant du Monomotapa Afhanglyk van Monohotapa.

Victoria, Couᵗ de l'Ordre de S. Dominique, KLOOSTER, van Sᵗ Dominikus.

Fort

Botong'a

J. Chingon, habitée par les Macuas, door de Macu as bewoond

Buento, ou on fait le Commerce de l' Or: daar de Goud handel gedree ven word

Chetuchin

Fatuca

Monomotapa, qu'on dit la Capitale de l'Empire, Hoofdstad des Ryks.

Cafres Independans ON-AFHANGINXE KAFFERS

Luaboel

Burro Mines d'Or: Goudmynen.

Forest de [Bosch van] Zebe

Em

Miticua Mines d'Or Goudmynen.

Berigo Jnhaquea

Bank van Sofala

Bon de [Bank van] Sofala

Rᵉ DE [KONINGʳ] QUITERVE

Sofala

ROYAUME DE [KONINGʳ] CHIKANGA

Zimbaoe

Riᵛ de Sofala

Sofala

I. Marovpe

Tierra de Quiloane

J. Isle Sainte, ou I. d

Manica, ou Magnica

Rᵉ D'[KONINGʳ] SABIA,

Rⁱ DE OU DE [OF] Sabia

Manbone

Anse d' [Inham] Asouca

J. Isles de [Eilan

Mines d'Or de Manica: Goudmynen van Manica.

SEDANDA

Tierra de Sogna

E. Sᵗ Sebasti

Riᵛ. Magnica, ou de Lawrent

ROYAUME D' [KONINGʳ]

Ave

Tonge

Botonga

Fort d' [Haven]Jnha

TERRES DU ROY [LANDEN DES KONINGS VAN] BIRI

Capricorni

INNANBOANE

Marquez

Tierra de Xembe

Riᵛ. Maumbe, ou de Sᵗ Christofle

C. Corientes, des Courans

Riᵛ. Tembe, ou du Lac

Querunde

J. Inhanga

LES [DE] HAINOUQUAS

Rio d'Ore Rio. de Spirito Santo, ou du Sᵗ Esprit

J. Inhapura

J. Inhaqua

Lac: Meir

Inhaqua

Longitude du Meridien de l'Isle de } Ferro. Lengte der Middaghlyne van't Eiland }

MONOMOTAPA

CHAPTER 1

THIRTY-NINE YEARS LATER.... ALAN BUNT'S JOURNAL AFRICA 1895

There was a time when I lived outside the reach of magic like most of us do, but I will tell you now a story that changed my life in a strange way.

It all began in the African Coast of Sofal in the area of Monomotapa where the river Manica and river Aroe converged the waters towards the Indian ocean.

As I recall it was a beautiful afternoon...
The Date December 18 1895...

A refreshing breeze whispered through the white verandah of Renzo's bar, cooling the sunbeams that streamed through seams of the umbrellas towering above the terrace.

As usual, for almost two years, the early afternoon saw me in the same west corner of the room where it opened onto the verandah. I was enjoying my solitude in my favorite rattan chair while drinking my Irish whiskey. The integration of the grandeur of the Victorian-style exterior of the building with the lush and tropical feeling in Renzo's had caught my fancy from the very moment I found it.

An acute rush of breeze kicked up dust from the terrace floor and slapped me as it blew by. My eyes lowered to my drink. I swirled the ice cubes around in my glass, emptied out the last drops of whiskey onto my waiting tongue and ordered another. I sat back and lit my cigar.

To my left, a large square mirror covered the wall, its border exquisitely etched with fine, swirling scrolls. The reflection of my movements to light my cigar caused me to look over, curious. Unconsciously, I adjusted the lapel on my jacket and came to the conclusion I needed to shave before my departure. I wouldn't consider myself an imposing man, but in some parts of the world, my 1.5 meter frame and 90 kg would make me a giant. I do have to admit, I thought to myself, that I have managed to stay fit in my thirty-nine years and was able to attract many a romantic glance from the opposite sex.

I brushed my brownish hair to the side in a feeble attempt to make myself more presentable—at least by my own standards; there was no one here who could possibly care.

I turned my gaze out over the terrace. This would be my last afternoon in Renzo's. My steamer would leave tomorrow for London, and reluctantly, I would be on it. Unhappy, frustrated, confused. I didn't look forward to the London winter, its dreariness compounding my failure. My quest had been fruitless and the many years of study and searching had been to no avail. I even questioned the sanity of my mentor Dr. Kruger…or his truthfulness…or my gullibility. He's the one who told me about the sacred **Sun Stone.**

Looking again at the mirror, I drifted into another daydream. I saw myself as a boy.

My mother told me that my father died when I was very young. I didn't really remember him or recollect what he looked like, so I can't really say that I miss him. When he died, my mother, Madeline Bunt, and I journeyed to London where she took on the responsibility of housekeeper for Dr. Walter Kruger.

Kruger's home was huge, but comfortable. Mother kept his house in the strictest order, though the doctor was gone much of the time. When he was home, he spent a great deal of time in his study, behind closed doors. It was the good Doctor's domain, so it was. On the first day we moved in, mother informed me that I was never to go into that room. So, as you might guess from then on, it was mysterious and held the unknown and it took all my will power to stay out.

Dr. Walter Kruger was a kind man, though he became pensive and seemed troubled at times. He always treated me with great love and respect, and received the same from me. I spent many years under his roof and I remember well the things he taught me. He talked about his travels extensively and consequently instilled in me a longing for adventure.

I hadn't even noticed that the hostess had brought me my drink. This time, I took my index finger and stirred. I licked my finger, then puffed my cigar before returning to my reminiscences.

I was ten, again. That rainy morning, I had been playing about the house, chasing a playful cat, when she decided to hide in Kruger's study. I saw her dart through that heavy, oak door which, usually shut, was left slightly open.

I stopped and remembered the warning. Never go into the study! Determined not to let the kitten have the best of me, I peered through the crack. It was dark and shadowy and I couldn't see the cat. I heard him taunting me, though, and he had to pay.

I swung the door open and pounced into the room, hoping to scare him from his hiding spot. I hadn't gone three feet when I tripped over something in the middle of the room, something hidden by the darkness. With a crash, I slammed into the floor, sliding across its polished surface. As I did, someone opened the drapes, causing the room to be flooded with light. My eyes quickly focused as I came to a stop, eye-to-eye with the most ferocious looking beast I could ever imagine. I squealed, instantly righting myself and backing towards the door, cat forgotten.

"I was frightened the first time I saw it, too," a deep voice said behind me. Startled, I turned to see a very tall and looming Dr. Kruger.

I slowly approached the horrid looking head that protruded grotesquely from the beautiful brown and black skin spread out behind it. It's teeth were yellowed, the eyes glistening mysteriously. "What is it, sir?" I looked up at him, trying to determine if I was in trouble for being in the study.

"It's a cape lion, Alan. I shot him the last time I was in South Africa. He had wandered into our campsite, looking for food. Oh, he probably would have become discouraged and gone on his way, but some of our guides fired a few shots at him, missing him but sufficiently angering him to retaliate. At the last moment, I had to put a bullet right behind his ear. See? Right here."

Dr. Kruger knelt down next to the lion skin, offering me his hand to come closer. I inspected the lion's head and sure enough, found the hole behind his right ear. I wondered if his frightening face had been frozen at the moment of death.

As I put my finger into the bullet hole, I asked what Africa was like.

Dr. Kruger paused and then stood. He walked across the study to his large, leather chair. It gave a rumble as he sat on it.

I didn't wait for an answer. "Did you have any other adventures there?"

"Yes, I made many interesting visits to Africa young man," Kruger began. "Indeed, it was during one of these visits that I heard a story about the existence of a kingdom full of riches and splendor. There is even a legend that this kingdom disappeared into thin air. The circumstances of this kingdom's disappearance seem to revolve around a sacred stone called the Sun Stone, a stone that holds magical powers. Years of research have given me good reason to believe in this tale, as wild and strange as it may be, I'm sure it exists."

The patient doctor stood and moved to a cabinet behind his desk. He reached in and pulled out a number of papers and maps, as well as a small, blue, velvet pouch, tied shut by a beautiful gold braid. He set the pouch to the side and spread out a map of the African Empire of Monomotapa, before me. My eyes were immediately drawn to the big red circle drawn around the western part.

"That is where I believe the Sun Stone is. Somewhere within that red circle. But I have never found it. Three trips there and not a trace." He rolled up the map.

"But, sir, if you can't find it, how do you know it exists?" I asked.

"Because of this," he answered. He picked up the pouch and untied the gold string and emptied something into his hand. He opened his palm to reveal a rock, smooth for the most part, but jagged on one side, as if it had been chipped from a larger stone. It was faded green and had some strange scratching on one side.

I looked up at the doctor with a questioning look on my face.

"I have reason to believe this is a part of the Sun Stone. With all my notes and years of research and exploration, this is as close as I have come to it."

"How did you get it? Who gave it to you, Dr. Kruger?" I was excited.

"Purely by accident," the doctor said. "It so happened that, sometime ago, I had gone into a small curio shop in Monomotapa. I was hoping to find a small memento of the trip for my late wife. As I browsed through the shop, I came upon this stone, lying in a round dish, with a few other odds and ends. I picked it up, and noticed a marking on it that very much resembled the hieroglyphics I had seen in papers relating to my research of the Sun Stone and the Lost City of Chandi, which is what I called the kingdom that was and is no more.

"I asked the curator if he knew what this stone was. He shrugged and mentioned that he got it one day from a beggar to whom he had shown pity. The beggar acknowledged his kindness by insisting that he take this stone. The curator said he hadn't thought much about it and only took it to rid himself of the beggar. He stuck it in his pocket, and when he emptied it at day's end, found the stone and tossed it into the dish. He had forgotten about it until now. I remember him saying that if I was so interested in it, I could just take it. And I did. Just this small piece gives me hope."

Dr. Kruger looked at me and recognized my excitement. He began to put the stone back into the pouch, and then stopped. Instead, he leaned down close to me and took my hand. He placed the stone in my hand and closed my fingers around it. "Take this. Someday, when you are older, maybe you will be able to find the Sun

Stone. If you believe, I think you will find it," he whispered.

Dr. Kruger grinned as he handed me the maps and other papers. "You take up the torch, Alan. Maybe you will have more luck than I".

"I will, Dr. Kruger, I will," I replied excitedly.

That was twenty-six years ago. And I'm no closer to finding the Sun Stone or any lost kingdom than I was that morning in Dr. Kruger's study.

I shook the memory from my mind; cobwebs that had gathered enough dust…and enough of my attention. Today was my last day in Africa. I looked hard into the distance, sipping my whisky, thinking how difficult it would be for me to finally say good-bye to this beautiful land.

As I tried to drown my dark and lonely thoughts, I noticed an old man crossing the bar floor. He was limping and was barely covered by his ragged, dusty robes. It was hard to see his face, as it was hidden by his matted and stringy hair. He was walking in my direction, slowly, dragging his left foot behind him. Once he reached me, he stopped and extended his open, shaky hand towards me. Surprised, but guessing as to his intentions, I reached deep into my pants pocket for some silver coins to give him.

He held up his hand to stop me and in a raspy voice mumbled, "I know how to find the Sun Stone."

A brief silence hung in the air as I considered this strange, out-of-place statement, wondering if my imagination had taken a strange turn. "I know how to find the Sun Stone," he repeated a little louder.

I blinked my eyes, bewildered, confused. My eyes made a cursory sweep of the bar; I was self-conscious, uncomfortable that someone might be watching this odd encounter.

I managed to utter, "The Sun Stone?" I looked closely at him, evaluating, trying to make sense of why this old beggar came to me with this information.

His eyes avoided mine, as if he felt guilty. He obviously shared my discomfort, and he, too, glanced about the room. He seemed preoccupied or in some kind of trance.

"Yes, the Sun Stone," he answered one more time, only with greater urgency. "It is only thirteen days journey to the West of the Lupata mountains."

Well, I had just spent almost two years West of these mountains and believe me, there was nothing there, at least nothing that my intense search had uncovered. I decided to grill him. "Who are you, old man?" I demanded. "Are you just begging for money. Are you trying to take advantage of me?"

"No!" he exclaimed hurriedly, putting his finger to his lips, asking my silence. "I've been looking for you. No one else."

His voice chilled me. He continued, "Find a man by the name of Chawa, in the village of Baratu. Find him and you will also find the Sun Stone."

He then extended his hand and this time his gesture was certain. Again, I reached into my pocket. Only this time, instead of drawing out silver coins, I produced a single gold coin, and pressed it into his hand, helping him close it around this precious token.

He thanked me, and bowed low, whispering, "If you believe, you will find it."

He turned and left Renzo's Bar. I watched him retrace his steps, limping slowly back to the front entrance. He never once looked back. He disappeared from sight as quickly as he had appeared.

My body felt tense; the pleasure I had found in my whisky had evaporated. Smiling to myself, I shook my head, picked up my drink and finished it. The sun began its dip into the horizon and though it was setting quietly for the night. It was a new day! A broad grin spread across my face. I wouldn't be leaving **Africa** just yet.

CHAPTER 2

BARATU

When the dense jungle finally opened, it gave way to a vast expanse of Blue Ocean. The refreshing, salty breeze was a welcome respite from days of suffering the jungle's humidity.

I paused to catch my breath and enjoy the view. I was standing at the edge of a very high cliff. I surveyed the area, looking for a path or road to the deserted beach below. I found none.

Below me, the Indian Ocean's gigantic waves heaved and broke violently on the white sands that were bathed with hot, blinding sunlight. Yet, there was a calm; a sense of Eden. I relaxed. This was a moment to savor.

Reenergized, I snapped back to reality. I knew that if I followed the deserted shoreline north, I would arrive, sooner or later, at the village of Baratu. Although my recent explorations had no reason to ever take me to Baratu, I knew that it was not far from Querunde, I had seen it on one of my Monomotapa maps dated 1750.

The best route to Baratu was north, along the coast. So, as I had done with regularity in recent years, I set out on foot, my maps, notes and clothes stuffed neatly in my satchel, to an unfamiliar destination—hoping to find the Sun Stone.

When I entered the village of Baratu, I was surprised. It appeared prosperous, at least by African standards, and certainly more than I had expected. Even so, it had only a single dirt "street," with small and medium-size shacks on both sides. Though Baratu's only street was not on the water's edge, as I had expected for such an "important" port, the activity was unusually brisk. The blazing sun fought a cooling breeze for control of the temperature—winning that battle most of the time. The sea was only a short distance; a pungent "fishy" smell told my nose the docks were only a few minutes away.

Barатu thrived. Hundreds of people bartered for vegetables and fruit at dirty, rundown shops. As I made my way down the street, a vacant lot to my left afforded me a clear view of the water's edge. Fishermen sat in their boats, jabbering among themselves as they repaired their nets or haggled with prospective customers. Everyone seemed to know everyone else.

There are so many people, I thought to myself. My search for this Chawa character might be a difficult task.

Where should I begin? I wondered. The railroad station? The village tavern? Now that was an easy choice.

I asked directions and was cautiously directed towards the far end of the street.

The sign announced "Linus One." As I approached the entrance, three drunken men were summarily ejected from the bar, two landed on their backs, the other tumbling head over heels. They were quickly followed by a huge, ugly man, who curled his fingers into a fist and shook it, angrily cursing these three good-for-nothings.

One of the men managed to stand. As he slapped dust from his torn khakis, he yelled back at the giant, taunting, "Forget you, Linus, you mindless ass. See if we ever come back to drink your watered-down swill."

He defiantly spat on the ground. He helped his two cronies to their feet and they staggered toward the docks.

I stood just inside the door to Linus One, impatient that my eyes were slow to adjust to the dark. Cautiously, I felt my way toward what I thought was the bar, trusting my thirst to lead me in the right direction.

The keeper leaned on the bar, talking to a girl. He didn't even acknowledge me, even as I plopped noisily on the stool. He deliberately ignored me, I'm sure. He continued to converse with the girl, their mumbling interrupted by the occasional giggle or laugh.

Finally, he shouted down to me, "What's it going to be?"

"Irish whisky, straight.... and two answers," I replied. I was too thirsty to care about his manners.

"Irish whisky?"

I didn't like his tone of voice.

"Listen, stranger, Irish is expensive...."

I pulled some silver from my pocket and tossed it on the bar. "I drink only the best," I said, a bit defiantly, if I do say so myself. I quickly flashed on Renzo's mirror, patting myself on the back for being so fit. "Bushmills, if you got it," tossing another silver coin onto the bar.

I had a bad feeling. Remain calm.... and alert, Alan, I thought.

The bartender came towards me, turning to say something to the girl, then reached under the counter. He stood up, holding in his hands an unopened bottle of Old Bushmills. He popped off the cork, and filled the chipped shot glass before me. I looked at it closely. Half worn away were the words "Sam O'Grady's Spirits Emporium. New York, New York." I chuckled.

He swept the silver coins into his hand. "This should cover about three shots." He returned to his lady friend.

I tossed another coin onto the bar, this one clattering with a different sound than the silver. The bartender immediately knew the difference. He stopped before the coin stopped spinning.

"This is for information," I said. "I'm looking for Chawa."

It was odd. He turned to me with the most surprised look. Then, catching his obvious reaction, quickly feigned indifference.

"Chawa?" he asked. "What's that? Some sort of animal, a fish?" He laughed, looking around at the other patrons who tittered approval of his sarcastic remark.

"I'm looking for a man named Chawa," I said.

"Ain't no Chawa 'round here," he mumbled and mindlessly wiped the bar in front of me. But he was listening, for sure. I could tell.

"No, ain't no white man in Baratu called Chawa," he repeated. "And I know most folks."

"I didn't say he was white. In fact, I don't know if he is and I don't care. I just need to talk with him. We have a mutual acquaintance."

I pressed. "Sure you don't know a Chawa?"

"No, but I might know someone who has maybe heard of him," he offered. Great!. I knew I was closer to Chawa.... whoever he was. All I really knew is that he had something to do with the Sun Stone and I couldn't pass up the temptation to investigate it.

"Wait here. I'll be back in a minute," and he disappeared behind faded, dusty curtains that served as the entrance to an even darker room.

After only a few moments, he returned, and was followed by the huge, ugly man that had earlier purged the bar of the three drunks. I was overcome by the now-too-familiar smell of fish, and it got worse as this hulk of a man got closer.

"You asked for Linus?" he demanded.

His breath hit me full force. By contrast, the fish smell was like a bouquet of roses. I shuddered and retreated a step, hoping to solve this very immediate problem.

"Not exactly, sir," I replied, straightening myself, trying to appear unpreterbed. The most gruesome smile spread across his face; a smile void of all but a few teeth blackened by the rot of inattention. His nose was bent to one side, the battle scars on his face attributed to his fights through the years. But his most obvious characteristic, aside from his breath, was his missing right eye. Its suppurating, empty socket made his face even more horrible to look at. When I saw it, I took another step back, this time from fear.

It had become strangely quiet, the dull mutterings of private conversation evaporated. Everyone there was watching this. How many were there? I looked around, but the corners were too dark to make any accurate evaluation.

Linus gave a deep, rumbling belly laugh. "Do I look like a sir?.... Sir! He sneered.

"Well, not really," I blurted before I realized my faux paux. "It's how I am accustomed to addressing strangers," I quickly followed, trying to cover my tracks.

"They call me Linus. Linus One is my name," he roared. "This is my place."

Again, his breath left me gasping for air.

"Yes, of course. Linus." I repeated and extended my hand. "My name is Alan Bunt."

Linus ignored my offer of greeting and walked past me. "I hear you're looking for someone. A 'Charna' or 'Chawa' or something like that." He looked at me with his one good eye and hissed, "What evil wind brings you here?"

Evil? What was he talking about?, I thought. "I'm looking for a man named Chawa. I was told to look for him in Baratu."

"You know him?" he grunted.

"No, but you could say I was referred to him. I've never met him."

"Oh, I'm sure of that," he interjected. "Nobody ever sees him. But I do know that if he wants to see you, he will find you first."

Without waiting for my reaction, he grabbed the bottle of Bushmills and took a long gulp. So much for me having another drink out of that bottle, I moaned to myself. But my thirst had long since vanished. Linus dangled the bottled between his callused, dirty hands.

He offered me the bottle. "Want another slug?" he asked.

"No. No, thanks." As the words caught in my throat, I raised my hands in protest. "I'm fine. I think I'll just be going."

"If Chawa hears that you are looking for him, and he will, he'll find you," he repeated.

I put two more silver coins on the bar and made my way to the front entrance, anxious to get away from this pit and back into the nurturing, albeit scorching, sun. Just as I reached the door, a voice shouted from a dark corner.

"Sundown. The Ovango waterhole."

I turned, squinting towards the direction of the voice. No one came forward. The patrons, now bored by my presence, had returned to their low, jumbled murmurs. Unable to locate the source, I just nodded in acknowledgment and left. Once back in the crowded street, I once again asked directions, and headed for the general store. The sun sailed high. I had plenty of time until sundown.

The Ovango watering hole was as deserted as it was remote—the villager from whom I asked directions didn't tell me it was so far. I had left right before sundown, but it had taken me about an hour to get here, and the last rays of sunlight had long since disappeared. I had my pistol out of its holster the entire time. This was not for the faint-of-heart.

I had the feeling that I was being followed, stalked from the shadows and cover of the bush. Along the way, I had been cautious, occasionally turning around to a rustle of leaves and sticks behind me. I stared out into the bush. It was impossible to see. Darkness comes quickly on the veldt and little time passes before it becomes alive with strange noises and stranger smells.

I had been walking for about an hour, concerned that danger lurked just around the next tree. But, for the past half hour, I had this feeling of being watched. It became more real as darkness overpowered the light. I hadn't seen anyone or anything. Thank God, no wild animals.

I stopped to take a big gulp of fresh water from my canteen. I allowed some to splash on my face, cooling it.

I was tired and sat down under a tree growing near the watering hole. Still holding my pistol, I leaned against its smooth trunk and took a deep breath and began to contemplate my decision to come here. Was I crazy? How could the lure of the Sun Stone be so great? I lit a match to check my compass and my map, wanting to reassure myself that this was, indeed, the right watering hole. Perhaps I should build a fire to keep the wild animals at bay. A good idea, I thought. But if a big cat was hungry enough, surely it would ignore the fire if it decided that I looked like dinner.

I laughed to myself. I felt foolish for being so nervous. After all, I did have my pistol.

I squeezed it, feeling more confident.

I laughed again, shaking my head in disbelief that I could be so paranoid. I put the gun back in its holster, and leaned heavily against the tree to wait.

After a bit, the jungle became very quiet, apprehensive. To my left, I heard the cracking of a dead tree branch. The bushes rustled. There was definitely something out there. Could be the wind, I rationalized. I was spooked and, before I could pull my pistol from its holster, the leopard pounced out of the bush towards me. His head thrust forward, jaws wide open. I panicked as he closed in on me.

I sat up like a shot and opened my eyes. Sweat drenched my shirt; I hyperventilated, gasping for breath, scared. Silence cloaked me. I glanced at my watch, finding that fifteen minutes had passed in a flash. Shaken, I realized that I had dozed off while sitting under the tree and had been dreaming. I also realized that I was no longer alone.

CHAWA

He was very dark and tall; almost as tall as the lance standing erect in his right hand. He stood perfectly motionless, except for the rhythmic flaring of his nostrils as he breathed. For a moment, I clearly felt as if he was walking around in my thoughts. Was he part of the dream? Was he a dream within a dream?

He had an imposing face; perfect features, as if sculpted from fine, black marble. His body was lean yet strong. His dark penetrating eyes were fixed on me, and behind them, the gleam of much knowledge and experience. I was impressed. And even though it appeared he was covered from head to toe in black, silky mud, I was not afraid of him. He looked at me and said, "You been looking for me?"

I jumped to my feet and started brushing the leaves from the seat of my pants. When I felt presentable, I stood straight and extended my hand in greeting.

"I'm Alan Bunt. I was told you could help me find the Sun Stone," I said in my clearest voice.

He stared at my extended hand for only a moment before he walked towards me. He came close, extending his hand. But instead of giving me the expected handshake, he grabbed my wrist. With his other hand he quickly and deftly wrapped a golden cord around my wrist and pulled it tight. I felt handcuffed! Bewildered, my first reaction was to pull away, but I noticed that he had an identical cord wrapped around his own wrist. I looked hard into his eyes. They were deep and mysterious, and projected a peacefulness I had never seen before. My body relaxed.

He suddenly spoke, quietly but confidently. "They call me Chawa. If you believe, follow me. I know the way to the Sun Stone you seek. It is thirteen days to the west. We must leave at first light."

Emotions heaved deep within me. I can't describe the feeling; it was one I had never experienced before, or have again, to this day.

Before thinking, and as naturally as can be, I nodded. "I do believe. I will gladly follow you to wherever you lead me."

I was surprised at my lack of resistance, as I am usually the cautious type, measuring my every move, my every utterance.

But for the first time in many, many years, I found myself leaping before looking. I blindly placed my faith in Chawa to lead me in the right direction. It felt right.

We built a fire in silence and then settled under the stars to sleep for the few hours left until daybreak. I stretched out under my tree; Chawa directly opposite me, sitting up under another tree, looking at me, barely blinking. Our journey was to begin shortly. It was a troubled sleep. I tossed and turned as dreams of what might come raced around in my head.

CHAPTER 3

13 DAYS TO THE SUN STONE

The sun doesn't get hotter as the day wears on; it begins its day full on, awakening everything in its view with a blast of heat, daring any creature to begin a days work.

Chawa and I set off to the West. He leading, of course, and I following, never questioning. There was rarely any conversation between us; Chawa seemed distant, in a faraway place—not of this earth. It wasn't that he was so strange but rather that he was on a mission of duty. Chawa was never threatening; he never became angered. He pushed on and on to the west, energy unbridled. I, on the other hand, had to stop occasionally to catch my breath or take a drink. Chawa seemed to understand and patiently indulged me as I recharged.

Africa is a continent of unchallenged beauty. It's called the Dark Continent because it is unexplored, for the most part, and its geographic wonders remain hidden from the civilized world. Over the thirteen days of travel by foot, I saw many incredible pieces of nature's wonders; mountains, waterfalls, trees, I'm sure have never been seen by anyone like myself, birds adorned with colors that brightly shimmered in the sun. Occasionally, a beautiful leopard or other beast ambled by, strangely going about their business, paying little attention to us intruding humans. That in itself puzzled me; it was as if they expected us and knew to leave us alone.

Except for the varying scenery or the steepness or difficulty of the trail, each day was the same. Everyday, we began at daybreak, picking berries and digging for roots as we went. Strangely, this sustained us and I was never hungry, though my stomach did growl or cry out for meat at times. We usually walked for six hours at a stretch, but I never found it in me to complain.

Chawa always stopped when the sun reached its highest point and insisted on dozing for about an hour. Then, like clockwork, he would bid me to continue resting as he would foray alone into the jungle. He was never gone for more than twenty minutes, and always returned with a skin full of fresh, cool water and four or five pieces of delicious fruit. We then ate in quiet, preparing ourselves for the afternoon trek.

This routine continued for twelve days. But I must say, that as we closed in on our destination, Chawa became even more quiet, more introspective. I had become quite sensitive to his actions and moods and, even if I hadn't counted off the days as we traveled, I would have been aware that the time was drawing near—the time when we would reach the Sun Stone.

When I awoke on the morning of the thirteenth day, Chawa was nowhere in sight. Believing that he was getting our food for the morning hike, I prepared for our last day on the trail. I extinguished the still glowing embers of our fire, and stirred the ashes.

After an hour, Chawa had not returned and I became concerned. But not knowing where we were or where we were to go, I stayed put. If anything can be said about me, I am not stupid. Chawa would return. I hoped.

Three hours passed. Finally, Chawa appeared through the brush. He walked rapidly toward me and I could see that he was sweating profusely and appeared to be short of breath.

"Chawa, what's the matter?" I queried.

He bent over and placed his hands on his knees, sucking in air, trying to catch his breath.

He looked up at me. "We are close to the Sun Stone. We must begin immediately," he directed. He then paused for a moment, as if it were an afterthought he asked, "Are you sure you are ready?"

A strange question, I thought. Why would he ask me that now? I did my best to keep my worries from Chawa.

"Well, I didn't come this far because I wanted to go on a nice hike," I said, trying to muster a laugh, mostly to diffuse my concern. "Yes. I'm ready."

CHAPTER 4

THE SUN STONE

There it was! Exactly where Chawa said it would be. At first it had sounded strange, seemed impossible, but true to his last word, the great Sun Stone now proudly stood right before our eyes! The sun's reflection over the water's surface surrounding the stone made it more interesting to look at; its changing colors over the smooth surface gave the impression of it being...almost...alive?

This stone rose from the middle of a calm pool of water like a single side of an ancient pyramid, shaped more like a quarter of a circle. The sun reflected off the water onto the stone, causing it to glow as if it were on fire. It was beautiful. More beautiful than anything I had ever seen. But was this the Sun Stone?

Beautiful birds, clothed in a dazzle of brilliant plumage, flapped their wings vigorously, flying around the stone, as if protecting it, in a display of territorial rights. Each had its own song, contributing to the symphony of sound that permeated the air. It was beautiful and fascinating. It tempted me so, that I began running toward it, unaware that I was doing so.

Suddenly, as if my action cued an orchestra, the rumble of drums filled the valley. Hundreds of drums, pulsing and threatening. The sound echoed throughout the valley, intensifying by the moment. The birds took flight, their beautiful songs becoming a cacophony of confused madness. The rumbling became louder and louder, surrounding us completely. Then, as suddenly as it had started, the drumming stopped.

Complete silence. No drums. No birds. For a few seconds, I stood completely still, listening. I heard only the pounding of my own heart, quickened with apprehension. I began to think I was going crazy. Was the drumming only a product of my imagination? Or was it real?

After gathering my wits, I again started towards the stone; only this time slowly, cautiously. I came to the edge of the pond that surrounded the stone as a protective moat. It was crystal clear and floating on its glassy surface were the largest and most richly fragrant water lilies I had ever seen. I looked down to discover that it was a shallow pond, one that could be forged easily. I took off my boots and dipped my foot

THE SUN STONE

in, the cool liquid and mud squishing between the toes of my hot and tortured feet. I waded in, testing each step. The bottom of the pond sloped down gradually, but the water never rose above my waist. As I made my way to the stone, I noticed the waves I was making caused the stone's reflection to shimmer and become distorted. I continued, and I soon reached the stone. I admired its perfection. It was 1.4 meters tall, and made of pure jade, softened only by the smoothness that time had worn into its surface. It rested on a pedestal of rough stone, cradling the round side of the stone, the point of the wedge pointing skyward, about 1 meter above the water's surface.

I circled the stone slowly, taking in its every feature, still wondering if this were the Sun Stone. It wasn't a round wheel, as the myth had said it was, and I suddenly thought I had been led on a wild goose chase… again. Just as I had almost completed my initial inspection, I came upon some writing on one side of the stone, etchings similar to hieroglyphics I had seen before. There were animal figures, kudu I think, as well as what looked to be springbok, elephants, leopards and, of course, monkeys.

Curiously, I found myself thinking that an icon like this would bring a pretty tidy sum from an interested party, whether it be museum, art dealer, or black market profiteer. I thought of Dr. Kruger, my mentor. If he could only be here right now, sharing this unique moment with me. I quickly inspected the Stone once more, and discovered a chip on the pointy end of the wedge. I fished into my pocket and pulled out the small chunk of rock that Dr. Kruger had given me many years before. I reached up and placed the smaller piece into the chipped area. It fit perfectly. I was overcome with emotion as I thought of Dr. Kruger.

With the excitement of this discovery, I had forgotten that I wasn't alone. Chawa. Thanks to him the Sun Stone became a reality for me. It was he who had led me to this place, the place to where I would soon bring my whole team to analyze this wonder.

I waded back to the edge of the pond. Chawa stood quietly, allowing me my moment of excitement. I smiled and waved to him. His piercing eyes looked through me, though, and beyond to the regal beauty of the Sun Stone. As I turned to look again at the stone, I realized that several forceful shots of water sprang from around the stone, as a fountain. The first sight of the stone had caused me to overlook this strange characteristic, and at that moment, I remembered something that Chawa had told me during our trek. He had repeated it only this morning as we set out for this final leg.

"If you drink from the water that springs forth from around the great Stone," he had said, almost chanting, "the Chandi doors will be opened for you and hence you will be able to enter the Valley of the Sun."

The first time he said this, almost two weeks ago, I ignored it; not putting much importance on it. But Chawa had repeated these same words twice now, as if to make sure I remembered them. His insistence on repeating them intrigued me, but still, I couldn't understand them. Now, I knew these words were important and that something extraordinary hid behind them, patiently waiting its moment for illumination.

I sloshed back out to the stone, and now, standing next to it, the water bubbled around me as his words ran through my mind. I looked down—the water was as clear as it was cool. I was tempted to take a drink but stopped. Chawa stood quietly watching me. I saluted with my hat and he acknowledged me, at least I think he did, with a brief crack of a smile, like as one a father would give a child who is obviously enjoying himself.

I spent the rest of the afternoon examining the stone, carefully letting my hands wander over its surface, pausing at each little engraving or inconsistency in its smoothness. The water began to get colder as the sun retreated to the west. I noticed that my skin had become wrinkled and white from too much time in the water. I became conscious of being tired, but my excitement hadn't waned for even a moment, and I continued to study the stone.

Chawa had began to make camp. He again followed his same ritual for marking out our space: a tarp held aloft by four uniquely engraved posts, each post at one of the four cardinal points of the compass. I never asked him why.

Finally, I had had enough, and reached up to remove the smooth chip Dr. Kruger had given me and tucked it deep into my pants pocket. I made my way to shore and dripping, strolled into the camp, Chawa was busily preparing the evening meal.

He looked up at me and said, "Let's eat. Then we will listen to the valley's chants."

"The valley chants?" I questioned. "What do you mean?"

Chawa ignored me, and filled my bowl with stewed fruit. We each found a rock to sit on, and ate in silence. I looked at Chawa carefully. He seemed more relaxed, more at home than I had seen him the previous thirteen days. His eyes appeared bright, they seemed to be smiling.

I turned my attention to the food. I was famished. As I ate I became aware of how tired I was. I set my half-empty bowl to the side, and stretched my arms to the sky, turning my head to hide a yawn. Yet, my mind raced, delighted with what had transpired that day.

I had been waiting for this day for thirteen years; years of research met with disappointment after disappointment. I thought back on the journeys I had undertaken to find this very spot, to enjoy the fruits of my labor, to validate my research. Yet, all the years of research and frustration had been forgotten by the entreaty of that raggedy old beggar in Renzo's Bar. How could this be?

I shook my head, and searched through my knapsack for my journal. With renewed energy, I began to enter my thoughts and feelings about the journey of the last thirteen days and the happiness and awe I experienced as I first ran my hands over the Stone.

I confided in my journal that I was not completely sure this was the Sun Stone, as its shape was not that of a large wheel. But, curiously, it could be part of a larger wheel. I just didn't know. I did know that the piece of stone the good Dr. Kruger had given me fit perfectly into the curious chip at the point of the stone, and the etchings on the small stone even lined up with the partials on the bigger wedge. My interpretation of the writing on the Stone, though, had almost convinced me that I had found it. But to what end?

Today was a turning point in my life, but, at the time, I had not realized just how much my life would ***change.***

The fire crackled and spat smoke to the sky, which was black and starless for the first time in our journey. Chawa had not said much, preferring to be content with his surroundings, the sounds and the smells. I do have to say that he had become more comfortable with me, considering that the first time we met was one of tension and suspicion. He never did say who he was and how he knew of the Sun Stone or why he had brought me to this place. I never asked. Yet, he seemed to warm up to me and sometimes I caught him looking at me with a knowing smile, then just as quickly avert his eyes from mine.

In the distance, I heard the persistent and strange sound that had followed us since the first day of our trip. This time, it sounded closer than usual, and more distinct. I turned to Chawa and, somewhat irritated I must admit, asked him what that strange sound was.

Chawa looked up. "Kratan!" he said.

"Kratan?" I repeated, haltingly.

"The Sacred Bird which guards the Valley. He is the Kingdom's messenger, accompanied wherever he goes by Konza, his faithful companion," he replied with matter-of-factness. Whatever was he talking about?

Although the sound didn't seem to disturb him, my question may have and he got up and moved away from me, going to the edge of the camp peering deeply into the jungle.

As for me, I was certain that the sound had gotten closer and seemed to take on an air of urgency. That disturbed me, but I questioned Chawa no further.

As I pondered Chawa's answer and his subsequent isolation, something huge passed over our camp, the air churning and violently whipping about me. I quickly unholstered my pistol, looking overhead. I headed in the direction in which this thing had gone. I came to a clearing about thirty meters from the camp to find a large kudu, a specimen of which I had never encountered. His eyes shone like burning sapphires in the darkness. His silhouette, barely illuminated by our campfire, was stark against the black backdrop of the foliage. The kudu was quiet, intently staring at me. Was it waiting for me? But wait! Something had flown over our camp, and kudus can't fly, can they? I thought to myself. What on earth had just flown over our camp? I turned as I heard a loud screech.

To the left of the kudu, perched on a tree stump, was a bird, as imposing a specimen as the kudu was. It looked like a crane, but was much larger, at least its body was larger than an ostrich's. Its' eyes were also illuminated, gleaming from the shadows, a fluorescent shade of emerald green.

However quiet and peaceful they seemed, this was not an ordinary occurrence, and without thinking, I followed my instincts and leveled my pistol at the kudu, drawing a bead on the center of his forehead. I began to squeeze the trigger, but before I could get a shot off, Chawa grabbed my arm, startling me.

"It's only the wind," Chawa calmly said.

Ignoring him, I again lifted my gun and aimed. But to shoot at what? I blinked, confused, staring at the drifting fronds of the tall trees. The shadows cast by myself and Chawa danced against the jungle curtain. The giant creatures had disappeared into thin air. Had they ever existed? I felt a mixture of anger and uneasiness, the peculiar sense of not being in control—a feeling that I hated. Why in heaven had everything that had happened lately seemed so extraordinary, so... so unnatural? For sometime, nothing had seemed to make any sense: not the old beggar, not the encounter at Linus One, and certainly not the relationship with Chawa, who had led me to this place. With every passing moment, I felt as if I were sinking in a sea of doubt. This whole tangle of circumstance and legend bordered precariously on the fantastic, tempered only by my refusal to view myself as insane and the reality of the jungle.

I cast these doubts aside when I thought of the Sun Stone. "Enough," I blurted, piercing the now silent stillness.

Tomorrow would come soon enough and there were things to do. But, for now, my only solace was the unfailing and loyal companion: the bottle. Its liquid fire burned my throat but soothed my tormented mind.

CHAPTER 5

CHAWA

Surprisingly, the next morning Chawa invited me to follow him on his hunt for food. I studied Chawa as he led, watchful and quiet as a cat. He constantly challenged my curiosity. He was tall, probably about 1.6 meters, and very lean, although his muscles were long and well developed. He had long burned off any fat that might have accumulated, as his diet consisted mostly of vegetables and fruits. He was covered from head to toe with a film of dried mud, probably applied as some sort of ritual. He was practically naked—he wore very little in the way of clothing, even when it became chilly in the night hours. Strangely, though, he always wore a fabulous pectoral, an interesting work of art depicting a sun encircled by series of stick figures and hieroglyphics, the likes of which I had never seen before, and a gold knife. His only other adornment was a bracelet of pure gold, just like the one he slid onto my wrist at our first meeting. I still wore it, I never asked Chawa about it, and he never told me why he gave it to me.

Strangely, though, he did unfailingly wear a fabulous pectoral, an interesting work of art depicting a sun encircled by series of stick figures and hieroglyphics, the likes of which I had never seen before and a gold knife.

Chawa had an aura of mysteriousness about him. His detailed physical features resembled none of the existing, indigenous tribes in the area (at least those I've encountered) such as the Zulu or the Xhoasa. His facial features carried such symmetry that it transcended perfection. There was no hint of vanity, just the opposite. His humble demeanor exuded strength and power. The truth is, I had come to feel comfortable around him, trusting. He carried himself—a person with a deep sense of inner peace, contentment and great wisdom. For the entire thirteen days of our trek to the Sun Stone I had seen him take things in stride, as if he had expected every obstacle, every challenge. What impressed me most was his harmony with his surroundings. He integrated seamlessly into his environment.

Because I was deep in thought about my fearless companion, Chawa's sudden stop startled me. Quietly, he put his finger to his lips, demanding my silence. He pointed to a clearing beyond. I slowly turned my head to see a springbok grazing quietly and ill-prepared for any danger. Chawa slowly positioned himself and, aiming carefully, forcefully blew a poison dart towards the unwary animal. Chawa's aim was true, and the point of the dart imbedded in the neck of the springbok. Surprised at the dart's sting, the springbok started toward us, angry and bellowing. It had gone three strides when its front legs buckled, and it hit the ground only a few feet from where we stood. We approached carefully. But the poison works fast, I thought, as the dying animal jerked suddenly and breathed its last.

Chawa pulled out his knife and carefully cut off several large strips of meat, enough to last us for a few days. We turned and headed back to camp, leaving the carcass to be shared among the jungle creatures that were certain to gather.

Back at camp, we prepared a fire to cook our meat. As raw meat would surely attract unwanted, yet very hungry guests, we cooked it all. The fire blazed, and the meat's pungent odor soon filled the air.

Looking at Chawa, I mustered enough courage to ask him a question that had troubled me since we met at the well.

"Who knows we are here, Chawa? We're not alone, are we?" I asked.

Chawa just looked at me, gnawing with relish a large, burnt chunk of springbok flesh. This was the first time I had seen him eat meat, and he was making the most of this meal. He watched me closely, and then, perhaps satisfied that he could trust me, nodded, spreading a wide grin over his face.

But no answer came from Chawa. He swallowed his last piece of meat, got up and, picking up what makeshift cooking utensils we had, calmly walked to the stream that meandered near our campsite. He washed things meticulously. Finished, he wrapped them in a dry piece of broadcloth I had and stuffed them into my backpack.

He turned and headed for the hill a hundred meters to the east, one that rose above the top of the jungle's roof only a few feet, allowing a superior view of the valley. He stood still for a few moments, then slowly spread his arms out from his side, and looked to the sky. He never released from that position as he first faced to the east, then the north, west and south, each time pausing for a few moments.

As Chawa went through his hilltop ritual, I found myself reaching instinctively into my pocket to make sure my precious shard of the Sun Stone was secure. It felt so smooth in my hand, and I rubbed it back and forth between my thumb and forefinger. After finding a quiet, shady spot to rest and write in my journal, it wasn't long before my eyes became heavy and I dozed off. I had angled my hat to shade my eyes from the sun, and nothing prevented me from drifting into nothingness.

CHAPTER 6

THE CAPTURE

An intense, stabbing pain in my stomach woke me from deep sleep. I hadn't finishing uttering my last "Ugh!" when my whole body began to feel jabs and pricks. While trying to get up, my hat came off, impaled on the sharp point of a primitive spear.When I had gathered my faculties, I looked up and found myself face to face with a group of unfriendly and fierce natives, who continued to prod and poke at me with their spears. Their short jabs were meant to subdue me, not kill me, and they laughed and jabbered among themselves as they continued to poke. I tried to defend myself by knocking the spears aside. Sensing impending doom, I reached across my body with my right hand to grab hold of my gun. A crushing blow from a spear shaft knocked me down. The last thing I remember was the ground rushing up to greet my face, and then darkness.

When I came to, it was nightfall. My head throbbed with a dull, constant pain. Although my eyes had not completely adjusted to my surroundings, I was aware of the bright, orange glow of a bonfire. As I raised my head from unconsciousness, I squinted towards the source of the light. About forty or so tribesmen danced and pranced around the largest fire I had ever seen. I tried to move, only to discover that I was bound securely to a sturdy post that was about a foot in diameter and buried deep enough into the ground that it wouldn't budge when I pushed against it with my back. My hands were tied together behind the post and my feet were entwined in a rope that appeared to be fashioned from some fibrous plant. Although I was still groggy, I knew I was in deep trouble.

I looked about me; no one had noticed that I had awakened. Everyone was obviously focused on the dancing and theatrics that was taking place around the fire. To my right, over a small knoll, a monkey sat quietly, chewing on something that smelled frightful, fruit maybe. It eyed me carefully.

Making its way to me, it offered me a piece of whatever it was eating. It seemed totally oblivious to the others, and, while I'm sure it was not aware of the precarious situation in which I found myself, I was surprised by its friendliness. Again, it offered me a piece of fruit. My hands being bound, I couldn't accept it.

THE CAPTIVE

It continued to eat, alternately spitting and chewing. Looking squarely at me, it bared its teeth and uttered a chattering string of monkey sounds.

One last time, the monkey held out a piece of fruit. I only could shake my head, refusing his offer. He tilted his head, first one way, then the other, examining me.

Unmercifully, my head continued to pound. Each time I closed my eyes then opened them, everything around me appeared blurry and cloudy for an instant, then slowly returned to focus.

I soon lost the little monkey's interest, probably viewing my not sharing it's food as an insult and he bounced away, in search of more responsive playmates.

I was determined to fight through my pain to make a full and accurate appraisal of my dilemma.

The native men continued to dance, a circle of women and children surrounding them, swaying to the beat of the drumming. I looked about the area for Chawa. Unable to locate him, I felt even more threatened. I hung weakly from the post.

I was pretty sure I hadn't broken any bones, but I could feel a few bruised ribs, and a lot of blood from the poking I had received earlier.

Then, for no explainable reason, I thought of my diary, my journal documenting the past thirteen days that had culminated in the discovery of the Sun Stone. I looked down, trying to see if its bulge was noticeable through the pants pocket in which I always kept it. Yes, it was still there, but I had no guarantee that it would not be found by these tribesmen.

Then I heard voices. Not familiar voices, but English voices. They seemed to be close by, and I looked to my left towards the sound, painfully twisting my neck and squinting into the dimly lit darkness. For a few, brief moments, I felt a renewed hope of salvation, that someone was there to rescue me from this terror.

I tried to lift my head enough to see them, slowly trying my best not to draw attention to myself. When I finally focused enough to see, I could make out two figures about ten meters away, standing in the shadows. Despair again surged through my being as I saw that they, too, were bound to posts similar to the one to which I was tied. I tried to get their attention, but to no avail. I had, however, caught the attention of my hosts. A sizeable group of my captors huffed and puffed as they walked toward me. I quickly focused, determined to be cognizant of whatever happened next.

These natives appeared to be in another world, maybe drugged, although I was aware that altered states of reality was a common occurrence in cultures in which dance played an intregal part in ritual. They spoke in an excited, clicking language that was unfamiliar to me. Many of them laughed and giggled, playfully shoving each other, daring retribution. I noticed that many of them were chewing on some sort of root or tree stem. One would tear off a piece with his mouth and hand the remainder to the man next to him, who promptly did the same.

They stopped and began to quarrel among themselves, occasionally pointing in my direction and then in the direction of the other two misbegotten souls. Apparently they reached an agreement and turned, en masse, in my direction. Again pointing and whispering.

Suddenly, a tremendous gust of wind blew recklessly through the clearing, fanning the fire and causing it to roar, as would a captured lion gaining freedom. A large amount of dust and leaves wrestled briefly and injected the air around me with a cloud. Birds seemed to fill the sky, their frightened screaming and crowing adding to the confusion.

The natives shrank back, looking into the sky, probably more frightened at the suddenness of this gale rather than the wind itself. Some ran for cover; others cried out and raised their arms to beg mercy from the elements; most stood still until it passed.

Determining that this brief tantrum of nature had ended, the group of natives again started toward me. I shuddered as I thought of becoming dinner for a tribe of ruthless cannibals. How painful a demise could one have, being dinner, I thought. I prepared for the worst, subconsciously spewing out "Hail Marys" as fast as I could. I sucked up some air and held it in my lungs, believing it to be my last breath.

The first one to reach me was an enormously fat man. He was so fat that his elbows and knees were nothing more than very deep dimples. He held a large piece of the root in his hand, and continued to chew, savoring every chomp. He held a small bowl into which he occasionally spat a disgusting green liquid, the residue of his chewing.

The natives gathered around me. The fat one held up his hand and immediately it became quiet. He cocked his head to one side and looked me over, up my body, then back down, as if considering what the best portion would be. It was then that a deep, baritone belly laugh rumbled from his lips, laughing uncontrollably, inciting the others to mimic him. A riotous laughter filled the air.

Again he raised his hand. Again, immediate silence. He turned away from me, and, knowing that he had the full attention of his backers, raised the cup of green liquid high above his head, as if it was an offering to some ancient god. He lowered it and turned to me, offering me the cup, insisting that I drink from it. I felt nau-

THE CANNIBAL

seous. There was nothing that would make me drink, even the threat of death itself. My refusal caused abrupt howling and chanting from the mob. To my left, my bound, English-speaking comrades gasped loudly, pleading mercy.

The fat native became incensed at my refusal to drink. He poked at me in a bullying manner. His pokes soon became severe blows. This whipped others into a frenzy. The whole crowd seemed to take one step forward, which only encouraged him. I became oblivious to the pain, each punch melting into the next.

Barely conscious, I managed one last thought, a pitiful "this is the end." I recoiled at my pusillanimous good-bye. Mustering up what courage I still had in me, I savagely dug deep to conjure up one primal defiance: "NOOOOOOOOOOOO!"

After the natives overcame their disbelief and initial shock at my wail, in unison they set upon me. The blubbery old "chief", or whoever he was, passed the cup of soupy spittle to the skinny fellow to his left. He reached out hard, grabbing me around the neck with such force that I felt for sure my trachea had been crushed. I gasped for air. Two quick slaps across my face forced my attention. Then, in a language from hell, he snarled a string of what I'm sure were unkind invectives, gave me one final punch to the midsection, and spat on me.

Oddly, again the camp was blown into a dust storm, an unusually chilly wind beckoning the flames of the bonfire skyward. This time, the unruliness subsided; the mob talked, no – mumbled, among themselves. Others pointed to the sky.

Even through my pain, I noticed the degree to which the temperature of the wind had dropped to an unbelievable iciness. The mob quickly dispersed, except, unfortunately, the fat chief and four others. The fat man urged my quick end, having been tempted by the smell of my blood. The others pointed at the two shadowy figures to my left, the English-speakers. The chief immediately forgot me and walked to the first figure.

The woman's agonizing screams held me fast to the situation, assaulting my pounding brain.

Blood dripped from a cut above my eye, soaking my shirt, mixing in with the sweat and dirt. Blood and perspiration clouded my vision, the salty beads burned my eyes. Everything again blurred before me, a result of my beating. I was struggling in that moment between twilight and unconsciousness.

I must do something, something to help....Again I shook my head, trying to clear it, hoping to rebound. The woman's screams begged my attention. I imagined their bruised bodies, hanging limp, unable to fall to the ground.

Two of the natives grabbed the man around the head and forced open his mouth. The fat chief approached and poured a good portion of the green slime into the man's open mouth. The woman screamed again. The natives untied the man. He bolted, running to nowhere, wildly choking and gagging. The newly formed crowd crowed approval.

The man ran toward the fire, obsessed, uttering an agonized scream as he disappeared into the flames. Please, God, take him quickly, I prayed.

The woman screamed and sobbed.

I wanted to cry out to her, to offer what sympathy I could. But the words stuck to my parched tongue. The savages milled around now, aroused by the smell of blood. My thoughts drifted randomly.

The villagers celebrated long into the night. It wasn't until the sun peeked into the new day that the village was quiet. For the moment, I had survived. So had the woman. Now if only we can both suffer through the heat of the day, I thought.

CHAPTER 7

THE JOURNEY

Merciless in its intensity, the sun tormented my eyes. What a terrible nightmare, I said to myself. I shook my head and squinted to survey the area.

The funeral pyre smoldered straight ahead. There was no one in sight, the village sleeping off a long night of celebration. It was already too hot to think about anything. I reached for my pistol—perhaps a reflex—only to find an empty holster.

Wait!

I looked down at my hands to suddenly realize they were no longer bound. Then, hearing a chatter behind me, I turned to find the friendly monkey holding out the twine that had shackled my hands. He stuck out his lip and started to make kissing sounds.

No time for thanks, I reached down and hastily untied my feet, and picked up my hat.

The woman was still tied to the post, her hands bound as mine had been. Her wrists were bloodied from her vain struggles. She had passed out in an awkward position, and her left leg was bent at a strange angle. If it wasn't broken, still it would surely be painful when she tried to stretch it out. She moaned as I worked on her bindings. I did it by touch, keeping my head up, sweeping the village, looking for anything that moved.

When she was free, she slid heavily to the ground.

In what might be our only chance to make an escape, I pulled the woman to her feet. Though somewhat shaky, she managed to stand. I quietly urged her to run as fast as she could, holding her at first. She stumbled for a few steps, then, amazingly, found her strength and stayed close behind.

We ran for almost an hour and I had no idea where we were. My adrenaline was spent and needed replenishment. I was ready to rest.

After about fifteen minutes, I began to think that the more space there was between the village and where we were could only be a good thing. I pulled the woman to her feet and we began again.

The jungle had thinned a bit, allowing sunlight to illuminate our path. We kept putting one foot in front of the other, for what seemed like hours. As we made our way through a clearing, the woman tripped and collapsed into a large clump of buffalo grass. I stopped and came back to her side. Her eyes were wide open, though there didn't seem to be much life behind them. I knelt down next to her, and brushed her tangled hair to the side.

Suddenly, a distinct sound fell on my ears. Water trickled nearby. Allowing the woman to rest in the safety of the grass, I made my way toward the sound and found a small pool hiding behind a thicket of tall grass. From it, a small creek ran down the hill into the valley below. I made my way to the water's edge, and feverishly splashed its coolness on my face, and satisfied my thirst. I lay there motionless, gathering energy. I stood up and returned to the woman, picked her up and cast her over my shoulder.

As we reached its edge, I staggered, lost my balance and we both fell, splashing into the pool. It certainly brought relief to our grime covered bodies. We languished for a few silent minutes, allowing the ripples to softly stroke us.

Finally, I turned to her, a bit surprised to find a lovely face washed clean by the waters.

"What's your name?" I asked.

"Elizabeth," she replied. "Elizabeth MacAlpine."

"I'm Alan Bunt," I said. "Listen. We have to move on. They might not be far behind." I stood and offered her my hand.

We headed down the hill, walking this time, following the stream. We had gone only about a kilometer when the stream disappeared under a huge, sandstone rock, blocking our way. We bore to our left around this monolith only to come upon the pool at whose center lay the Sun Stone. It glistened in the noon day sun, the fountains of water spouting around the stone.

Familiarity flushed through my body. Was this coincidence, I thought to myself? Again, I felt the energy of the Stone pulling me, beckoning me to its side. Its beauty, in the middle of this placid pond, was in stark contrast to the terror we had experienced last night.

It was then I thought of Chawa. I wondered what happened to him. It was surely strange that he would just disappear.

His words intruded into my thoughts:

"If you drink from the water that springs forth from the great Sun Stone, the doors of Chandi will be opened for you and hence you will be able to enter the

Valley of the Sun."

I cupped my hands and lifted a double handful of pond water to my lips. I urged Elizabeth to have a drink. Without hesitation, she leaned over scooped up a drink.

I waited a few moments, expectantly. But I didn't feel any different, and certainly no doors had been opened.

I again ran Chawa's words through my head, searching for some small clue.

"If you drink from the water that springs forth from the great Sun Stone, the doors of Chandi will be opened for you and hence you will be able to enter the Valley of the Sun."

We each took another drink. Nothing. I looked around.

No doors, I thought. It was a nice try, anyway.

I turned my attention away from this foolish magic as Elizabeth sighed with fatigue. Although the fates had thrown us together, I knew I had to quell my curiosity about my new companion. My eyes wandered full circle about the shore line. I looked hard for the place where Chawa and I had camped earlier. How long ago was it? The cannibal experience had clouded my sense of time. Certainly the campsite would still be there. And perhaps some of the supplies that Chawa and I had brought with us.

No such luck.

I felt alone but made certain that I didn't show it to Elizabeth. The discovery of the Stone offered little solution to our present need: a place to hide for the night. It would be terrifying enough in this remote, wild area, and a fire of our own was out of the question. We didn't want to set up a beacon for the savages, who must be pretty upset by now. Considering this very likely possibility, I turned to Elizabeth.

"We must move on. There isn't a moment to spare." I didn't have to try to sound urgent.

We headed into the valley, silently as possible, searching for adequate, camouflaged shelter.

We came upon a large waterhole. A large family of elephants were enjoying a family bath, alternately spraying each other with water and rolling around in the mud. They ignored our presence.

We continued on. The afternoon sun slowly made its way west and a cool breeze swept across the valley, coaxing many rested wild animals from their lairs. We saw herds of zebras, who were the most curious. Some even followed us for a while, watching, wondering. A few kudus crossed our way—but none as large as the one I thought I saw a few nights ago; the one with the sapphire eyes. The shrieks, baring of teeth and threatening lunges from a large family of baboons frightened Elizabeth.

"I really think the baboons are only trying to chase us from their territory. If we pretend to ignore them, they'll probably leave us alone," I told her, fairly certain I was right.

With a renewed spirit, we forged ahead. But not for long.

"I can't go on anymore," cried Elizabeth. "Let's stop."

We found a large pile of stones that cast a large, cooling shadow. We both dropped to the ground and sat silently.

After a period of time, I was alerted by a slight movement. In the distance, a pack of hyenas wandered back and forth, spying about the area. For the moment, I wasn't concerned as they seemed to be unaware that we even existed.

But they continued toward us, and the yelps and howls became uncomfortably close. Now, I could tell they were many. Elizabeth sensed my alert, and spotting the hyenas, screamed out in alarm. The hyenas stopped dead in their tracks, then quickly retreated to assess the situation.

Great, I thought to myself. Now they know we are here for sure.

"Quickly. Leaves, dead wood. Anything for a fire," I directed. Without saying a word, Elizabeth quickly grabbed a handful of leaves. I reached into my pocket and found two matches, both wet from my wade to the Sunstone. No fire.

The hyenas had evidently made the assessment that we were going to be easy prey as they again approached us, but not as cautiously.

"Stones!" I shouted.

We began to throw in the direction of the pack as fast and as hard as we could. It was easy to tell when a stone found the mark. We continued our defense and the hyenas again retreated to reconsider.

Elizabeth swung around and looked past my shoulder.

"Look! Up there!"

Our stony protection was at the base of a sharp slope that rose suddenly out of the ground. At the top were two dark areas; they appeared to be caves.

Without a word, we set up the hill, clawing our way to safety…we hoped.

I reached the cave first and turned to pull Elizabeth up the slope. She crawled on her hands and knees into the left cave. I was close behind, hoping this wasn't a lion's cave.

CHAPTER 8

SAFETY

A particularly brave hyena had gotten close enough to nip at my heels. I kicked at him, and caught him in the snout, but he persisted and got a grip on my pant leg. Elizabeth threw a stone the size of my fist, hitting the snarling animal's head, sending him yelping in retreat.

"Quickly. Help me block the entrance," I shouted, scrambling into the cave. Elizabeth and I spent the next five minutes silently building a barrier across the entrance. Leave, rocks, sticks, whatever we could find. I put one large, sturdy stick to the side to use for a weapon. It was pointy enough to discourage any attacker.

After the barrier was erected, Elizabeth and I sat quietly, catching our breath. The cave was dark, and my eyes still struggled to adjust to it. It was eerily quiet, only the sound of our heavy breathing touched my ears. I could barely see Elizabeth sitting across from me. Time slipped by.

As the sun fell farther from the sky, more light filled the cave, as there were a few cracks in our rocky refuge that opened to the west. This light, though, would soon be gone.

I looked around, then looked above me. The rock formation was an odd one; a grouping of boulders piled high as if by some god to be used as a marker. That left plenty of ventilation. We must build a fire. If only I had matches. Dry matches.

"Maybe we should build a fire," Elizabeth said, as if she had read my mind.

"That would be nice," I agreed. "But how are we going to light a fire. I had two matches, but they are no good. They got wet at the pond."

Elizabeth reached into her front pocket and pulled out three wooden matches wrapped in a small piece of oilcloth. Dry matches. After such a string of bad luck, it was hard, at first, to accept this bit of extremely good luck. We gathered together a bit of dry kindling and I lit one of the precious matches.

The fire sputtered to a start. I prayed that it wouldn't go out. I didn't want to use another match. I carefully placed some more leaves on the growing flames. I nurtured it to a fire that would be more than adequate.

Elizabeth stared blankly at the fire. "Light is a miracle," she said in a monotone.

She must have sensed that I concurred.

I wondered about the hyenas. I wasn't quite sure if they had gone on to less challenging prey, or had simply retreated for a rest. I crawled to the barrier we had constructed and removed a few of the top stones so I could look out.

I could look out over the entire valley from this vantagepoint. Under different circumstances, I might have paused to admire the view, to consider the perfection of God's creation. But I was in no mood.

Waning sunshine bathed the tops of the trees and the distant mountains. A sheet of somber grayness was being pulled slowly over us from the east. The tiny daggers of sunset streaked across the sky, swallowed by the approaching night. Its magnificence demanded pause. Silently, I acknowledged its grandeur, but it wasn't too long before my thoughts drifted to Elizabeth and our task at hand. The task to *survive.*

CHAPTER 9

ELIZABETH

Elizabeth changed positions and moaned. I looked over my shoulder to see her massaging the leg that had been awkwardly bent back at the cannibals' camp. I put back a few of the rocks I had removed from the barrier and crawled back to my spot.

I stared at Elizabeth, really looking at her for the first time. She was quite attractive. Though it was somewhat dirty from the work of our escape, a mane of golden hair framed her face. I could tell that it was naturally curly and, under different circumstances, would cascade wonderfully onto her shoulders. Her blue eyes were like finely polished gems—rare and captivating. She fought to stay alert. The day's blazing sun had significantly reddened her cheeks. Her bottom lip pouted naturally, complementing her full upper lip. Actually, quite attractive doesn't do her justice. She was beautiful.

She was petite, very shapely but very lean. She had to be in superb physical condition to survive what the past 24 hours had offered.

She became uncomfortable at my obvious assessment. Her eyes purposely avoided mine as she nervously pushed her hair from her face. Her sleeve pulled back to reveal a shiny, golden bracelet on her wrist. It was a band quite similar to the one Chawa wore, and the one that Chawa had thrust on my wrist when we first met.

My thoughts wandered back to Chawa. I still couldn't make sense of his disappearance. I gave him up for dead.

Realizing that I was tired, I shifted about, trying to find some degree of comfort, then I succumbed to sleep.

I hadn't slept for too long before the chill of night began to fill the cave. The sun had already dipped past the edge of the earth. The smoldering fire begged to be fed, and I quickly broke some sticks and placed them on the embers. They were so dry they quickly burst into flame. The darkness of the cave diminished and I saw Elizabeth huddled farther back in the cave, sobbing quietly, but uncontrollably.

I called out to her. "Elizabeth."

ELIZABETH

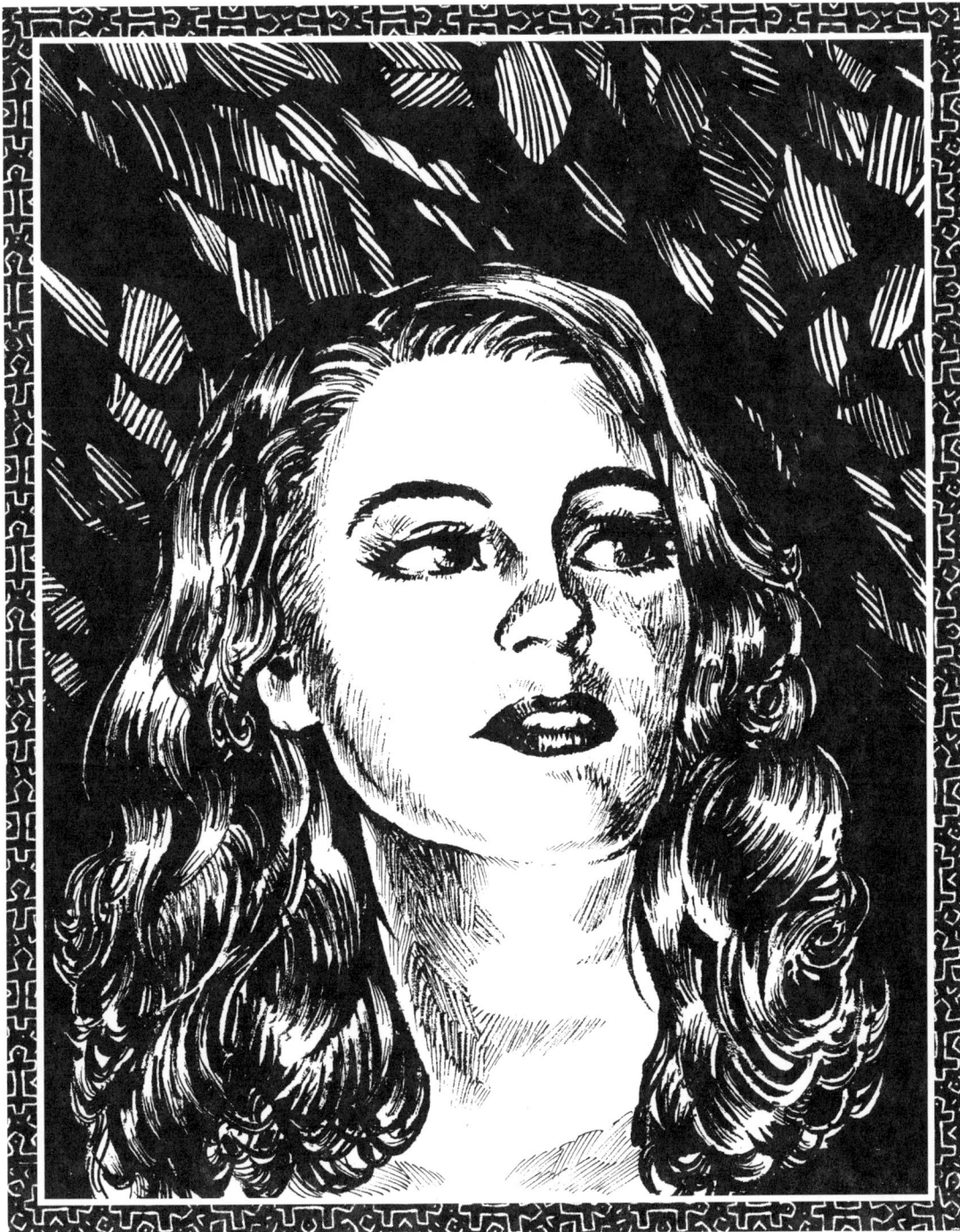

Her sobbing ceased and silence followed.

"Everything's going to be all right. Don't be afraid. Please, don't be afraid," I pleaded.

I spoke in measured, soothing tones. I tried my best to be a calming influence. "Please," I continued, "let me help you."

With these words, she began to sob uncontrollably. I hesitated, feeling helpless at her distress. Although we were complete strangers to one another, I went to her and held her. After a while her tears stopped and she settled in close to my side, shivering violently. Instinctively, I rubbed her shoulders as my thoughts wandered back to the incredible events that had brought us together in this cave. As I felt her calming, I glanced down, surprised to see her looking at me with eyes full of questions.

I took my time. "I had a guide. Chawa. The last time I saw him was when our hungry hosts raided our campsite back at that lagoon. The one with that beautiful Sun Stone in the middle," I offered. "But I haven't seen him since. I don't know if he's dead or alive."

"He abandoned you?" she quizzed.

I shrugged. "I don't know. I do know for sure that I didn't see him at the village."

"Maybe they killed him," she pressed.

"Maybe," I responded, " but somehow I don't think so."

Chawa was far too clever to become some wild man's main course. He obviously knew the area well, and I doubt that he would have left himself vulnerable to that kind of danger. He was too measured, too careful, though he never mentioned the possibility of cannibals to me. Maybe he was one of them. No, no, I thought. How absurd.

I prayed that he escaped and went for help. As for me and my bruised and battered partner, we needed to make a plan.

I thought about the Sun Stone. It was the most significant discovery I had stumbled on in my entire life. However, the dangers Elizabeth and I now faced put the Sun Stone in the recess of my mind. I knew then and there that we must leave at first light to try to find our way to Baratu, back to safety. Hopefully, my business partners and fellow researchers had become concerned at my prolonged absence. Perhaps a search party had been formed and had begun to look for me. But how could they find me? As far as I know, only my "friend," Linus, the Barutu bar owner, really had an inkling of where I had gone.

I shuddered at my next thought. Even if a search party, ended up in Barutu—at best a remote possibility—they wouldn't ask the likes of Linus if he had seen me. And he wouldn't tell them that he had. I was certain of that.

My eyes drifted down Elizabeth's body and again fixed on the bracelet circling her right wrist, which rested on her thigh. I had to ask her.

"Please tell me how you got your bracelet. How did you end up at the village?" I gently prodded. I lifted my right hand and shook it.

"See? I have a bracelet, too. I got mine from Chawa. Where did you get yours?" I whispered.

She then told me her story.

"John Sutton was my fiancee," she began. "He had been studying ancient African cultures. He had just about completed his research when he came upon an old scroll that contained a story, the legend and legacy of someone called the Sun King. How John came to possess this scroll is strange enough in itself."

Elizabeth arched her back and allowed her head to fall backwards. She moved her head from side to side, stretching her neck muscles as she massaged her neck.

"John had taken a short excursion to a small village along the Tanganyika Lake and he met an old medicine man that spoke of this mysterious leader: the Sun King. As John told it, the witch doctor led John into his thatched hut to a wicker chest. He opened it. There, on a pile of golden coins, lay the scroll, the history of this Sun King. The old man reached into the basket and retrieved the scroll and two of the gold coins. He handed them to John and then ushered him quickly from the hut.

"John was so excited. He immediately returned to London and came to visit me and my father, Sir Alfred MacAlpine, who was a retired Foreign Service worker for His Majesty's empire. My father served many years in Africa and came to love its mystery."

"I remember my father stared in surprise when John told him of the scroll. He immediately poured two glasses of brandy, handed one to John and sat him down. He then went on to tell John that during one of his tours of duty in Africa, he was lucky enough to gain an audience with a Zulu chief who related a similar story about the Sun King. My father asked the chief to elaborate, but the chief quickly dismissed him, realizing that perhaps he had given away a dark secret. My father had filed the story away in the recess of his mind, and hadn't thought about it until John's story unlocked this faded memory.

"John and my father quickly formed a partnership and headed back to Lake Tanganyika, to learn more about this legend of the Sun King. As my mother had died years earlier, my father had made it habit to take me wherever he went. Now, he had it firm in his mind that John and I were to be married and, as I wasn't particularly taken with John, I resisted for a long time. Respectful of my discomfort with my father's plans, John kept his distance, while he and my father immersed themselves in research, learning more and more about the Sun King. To keep busy and put myself to some good use, I acted as their assistant. Of course, this meant being around John every day and it wasn't too long before John's character and brilliance allowed me to acquiesce to my father's matrimonial plans."

By now Elizabeth and I were surrounded only by the glow of our fire as darkness had long decended on the valley below. An occasional shriek from some distant sector of the jungle was always met with some reply at the far end of the valley. The cover of darkness is of little help in the jungle and all in all, I was more comfortable being in here than I would be out there.

Elizabeth continued. "After several months, my father was recalled to London and he announced that enough research had been accomplished that we should all return to London together.

"John was not enthusiastic about that prospect. He insisted on staying to continue his work, saying that my father and I should go alone.

I simply could not return to London leaving John's side. Only after I had become engaged did father relent and allow me to stay because he would return shortly.

"John and I were anxious to begin looking for the Kingdom of Chandi…"

Chandi, I thought, trying to recall Chawa's saying. The doors of Chandi?

"…so we immediately began looking for a guide to take us to Bulawayo. We found three stout men to carry our equipment through the jungle."

Elizabeth snuggled closer. It was getting chilly.

"After two days, we reached the great savanna, and we found ourselves surrounded by an abundance of fauna, arousing the hunting instincts of our escorts. In that single afternoon, they had slaughtered three large animals. More than enough food. We made camp there, and, between stories of greatness and bravery, we ate and drank. Soon sated, we all drifted into sleep."

I stoked the fire, but it was getting smaller and we had used up practically all of the fuel. I placed the last twigs and leaves on the flames and they burst quickly into a last bit of light and warmth. I tore a few precious pages from my journal (blank ones, of course!) to gain us a few more moments of light.

"The next morning, John and I awoke to a deserted campsite. The escorts had absconded with our supplies sometime during the night, leaving us nothing but our guns and ammunition. I remember John and I wondering about the fact that they hadn't taken our guns. But they did take our food and medical supplies. As John was familiar with this territory, we weren't too alarmed, and calculated that we could reach Bulawayo on our own by dusk the next day if we kept a steady pace. We walked all day and slept peacefully that night."

Tears began to well up in her eyes as she reminisced.

"But how did you come to be captured by cannibals?" I gently urged her to continue.

"The next morning, we got up and prepared to depart on our final day's walk. Suddenly, out of nowhere, a very tall, practically naked man walked toward us. John's instinct was to grab his rifle. The native stopped and raised his hand. He was wearing the most incredible pectoral, and the early sun glanced sharply off of its gold plating. He wore a bracelet like this. We tried to determine his tribe. His features resembled those of the Jacurs, but somehow too chiseled. He also had a quiet mystery about him—an air of confidence. He was covered, head to toe, in a second skin of mud. He calmly approached us. John and I clung to each other, taking a few steps back.

"His eyes were so penetrating. He stopped right in front of us and said in perfect, unbroken English, 'You are to keep this bracelet with you always. Do not take it off. You must believe. It is very important that you believe.' John and I looked at each other. The tall man reached out and grabbed my right hand, and slid this bracelet onto my wrist. Without saying anything further, he turned and disappeared into the thicket."

"Sounds like Chawa," I offered. But how could that be, I thought to myself. Chawa was with me.

"John and I were so stunned. I lifted up my hand and we both carefully looked at the bracelet. It was so mesmerizing that we didn't even notice that we had suddenly become surrounded by those ruthless, horrible cannibals. We were so quickly set upon that John was unable to aim his rifle. The blow of a spear shaft knocked it from his hand before he could get off even one shot.

"We tried to communicate with them, trying every language and dialect we knew. Failing at that, they made it very clear to us that we were to follow them. John persisted in his attempts to talk with them. They only grunted and offered us some dried meat. It smelled too horrible, and we both refused. But I did have some water, against the entreaty of John not to sip what might be poison.

"The heat and the flies pestered us relentlessly. We walked for hours, and it was early the next morning before we came to their village. Our captors were received like heroes returning from a war. After being paraded about for what seemed like an eternity, we were tied to the posts, and left alone to contemplate our fate. Several hours later, you arrived.

"You were carried by four of the younger natives, and they were joined by two others as they bound your hands and feet to the post. Two native boys, not more than twelve years old, followed behind with what appeared to be some of your personal belongings that they felt would be useful to them. In one woven box was your hat, and the smaller of the two boys snatched it up and placed it on your head. He followed this with a punch to your stomach."

I shuddered as I thought back. How long ago was that? I still was hazy about time.

"You know the rest, I believe," Elizabeth sighed.

"Enough of this." She sat up and faced me. "This is all a terrible nightmare. I keep pinching myself, believing that I might snap out of this dream. I'm hungry and there's no food. I'm thirsty and we have no water. My whole body aches, my feet are solid blisters, and those hyenas lurking about outside are probably making a plan. On top of all that, I still expect a crazed cannibal to suddenly appear and recapture us. I'm beginning to think I'd be better off if I had followed John into his fiery tomb."

"No." I tried to sound confident. "We still have a chance."

We were quiet for a long time. Elizabeth's breathing became deep and even. Finally, she had been able to fall asleep. I could not. Just as well, I thought. Someone has to stay awake.

I crawled once again to the mouth of the cave and positioned myself so I could see any approaching danger, at least as far as the darkness would allow. I pulled my pointed stake close to me. Nothing seemed threatening at the moment, although the night was filled with the symphony of the great savanna. Small animals scurried to their hideaways.

I inhaled deeply, filling my lungs. The smell of the wild drifted under my nose. Feeling a bit more at ease, I removed two more rocks and some bushes from the mouth of the cave, placing the rocks close enough to be used as projectiles, if I needed them. The moonlight graciously illuminated the jungle below, but the air was heavy and stagnant.

In the darkness, Elizabeth awoke and called out. "Shall we take turns keeping watch?"

Her offer reminded me of how she had tried, all day, not to be a hindrance, a burden. Her silence hung in the dark as she waited my answer.

"It's all right," I said. "I'll stay here at the entrance a bit longer. I want to be sure we are safe. Go ahead and sleep. I'll be fine. Daylight is not far, so rest."

I wondered again at the separate paths that had brought both Elizabeth and I together. The memory of her fiance running into the cannibal's flames came back to me. That Elizabeth could endure the loss with such bravery fulled me with admiration for her, and with caution for the feelings that had begun to emerge…John had been a very lucky man… .

I pushed the thoughts and images away.

It couldn't have been a half hour until I, too, fell asleep. Two tired humans: the protector and the protected.

CHAPTER 10

THE CAVERN

I awoke to the sound of rocks clunking on the cave floor. Elizabeth had come to the cave opening, removing more rock. She peered out, cautiously. It was almost dawn, and the cave began to lighten with each passing minute.

Elizabeth turned to me.

"Good morning!" she said, with shy familiarity and a welcome smile.

"I sincerely hope so," I joked. "What's your hurry? Have you erased yesterday from your pretty little mind so soon?" I rolled my eyes. What a stupid thing to say, I thought. Pretty little mind? How disrespectful.

"No, of course not," she answered, apparently not registering my blatant chauvinism. "I think it's safe."

"Well, you can't go out there. Not yet, anyway," I chuckled.

I got up and walked, stooped, to what I thought was the end of the cave, a perfectly private spot to relieve myself. I noticed another passageway shooting off to the right. Curious, I looked harder, wondering if I had found another entrance to, or exit from, the cave.

I called to Elizabeth. No answer. Again I called. I turned and made my way back to the now semi-barricaded entrance. Elizabeth sheepishly crawled over the barrier back into the cave.

I glared at her accusingly.

"I'm sorry, Alan, but Nature makes her demands," she explained. It was then that she noticed the puzzlement on my face.

"Come quickly," I beckoned. "Come check this out...."

I handed her the pointed shaft. "Use this if you see anything strange."

Without another word, she followed closely behind me. It was dark and we felt our way slowly.

This was no good, I thought. I can't see a thing. I stopped and reached into my vest pocket and pulled out my journal. I opened it and tore out a few blank pages. I rolled them up, tightly, and turned to Elizabeth.

"May I have one of those matches?" I asked. We had two left.

I lit my makeshift torch, but it was still hard to see. We penetrated farther down the passage way, the little flame barely lighting our way. We slipped and slid down several sharp inclines, the loose sand hurrying us on our way. After sliding down a third slope, Elizabeth became frightened and wanted to go back. I grabbed her hand and continued on. As we rounded a sharp corner, we were met by a stone wall. As abruptly as we came upon it, my torch fizzled out.

"Oh, God," a very distressed Elizabeth said. "Quick, light another."

I felt for my journal, and opened it. I tore out a number of sheets and fashioned two small torches. Our final match burst into a flame long enough for me to light the papers.

Light flooded the chamber and the wall before us. Was this the end, I wondered? In frustration, I pounded on the wall and kicked at its base.

Amazingly, a stone door to our left swung open. Elizabeth and I looked at each other and headed through the door.

A quick rush of air quickly extinguished our torches, scattering the ashes, and we were left in the darkness. But not complete darkness.

We cautiously made our way toward a faint light and found ourselves at a ledge that overlooked an illuminated pool, fed by water that seeped through the walls. It was humid and unusually warm. To our left, a path dropped to the pool, lined on both sides by lime cones formed by dripping, liquid minerals oozing from the caverns ceiling. It was eerily beautiful. We slowly made our way down the path to the water's edge. Light filled the cavern, but we could not determine its source. It was just there.

We continued around the pool, faithfully staying on the path, until we arrived at the other side. The path led us still further, around a corner, and then another. It seemed as if we were always turning to the left. After about five left turns we entered another illuminated cavern, one of even greater spaciousness and grandeur. Elizabeth and I stood, hand in hand, our mouths agape, our eyes beholding magnificence.

THE TEMPLE OF RAJUN

THE TEMPLE OF RAJUN

Its indescribable beauty impressed me beyond words. We had just entered a subterranean palace, supported by columns of unimaginable coloring. Its size was immense, and its shape was perfectly oval, as if scooped by a god's spoon. Its hollowness amplified the drip of water. How could such a place exist? The cave into which we sought protection yesterday was so nondescript. There were no clues that it was an entrance to anything more than a resting place for some tired animal. Or a refuge for frightened people.

The crafted, colorful pillars stood boldly, strengthened by time and washed in the most illuminating colors. This couldn't be the result of Mother Nature, I thought. Surely some of this was planned, was built by human hands. Maybe we had stumbled upon the remains of some ancient culture, I thought. I had reached a point when nothing could surprise me, especially after the last few days.

A pool of water had collected on the cavern floor. The entire circumference of the pool was separated from the cavern walls by a few feet of dry land, most overgrown with lichen. In the middle of this pond was an island. There was nothing special about this island except that, in its exact middle, a brightly-illuminated pillar—a monolith—rose proudly into the air seven meters or so.

We made our way to the pond's edge, staying close to the wall. We came to a spot where seven white, smooth rocks poked their heads above the calm water. Each was carefully spaced about a half-meter apart and connected our outer walkway with the island. Elizabeth and I hopped from stone to stone. Seven stones. Eight hops. Curiously, to the right side of the stones the water was calm and uncommonly clear; to the left, the water was cloudy and murky and I couldn't see the bottom.

We reached the island and immediately went to the pillar. It was probably ten meters in diameter and was a perfect cylinder, standing on end. I gently slid my hand across its surface. It was cold to the touch but smooth as satin. Up the side of the pillar was a fascinating stairway that corkscrewed to the top. I took a few steps back and looked up, but could not see the top. I ran to the foot of the stairs, followed closely by Elizabeth.

Bounding two stairs at a time, we made it to the top in short order.

Suddenly, I realized that I was dead center in the middle of the cavern. I got the feeling I was suspended in the air.

We cautiously walked to the edge of the cylinder and peered carefully over the side to see the island below. The sheerness of its sides caused us to recoil and retreat quickly.

We both turned to the center of this pillar, from which rose another stone, much smaller, about a meter and a half. It, too, was round, like a table, and was about two meters in diameter. A shard of jagged crystal erupted haphazardly from its center. The obtuse angle at which this beautiful crystal emerged from the stone's center was in sharp contrast to the simple, straight forward design of this monolith and the altar before us. The light captured by the crystal arrayed against the ceiling of the cavern.

On the table top, starting next to the crystal and spiraling out to the edge, familiar pictures and runes had been chiseled into the face of the top of this smaller stone. The spiral continued down the sides and eventually onto the floor, or the top should I say, of this huge cylinder. There were a few drawings that I had come across in my research. They were primitive and offered little clue as to what this monolith was or what it was for.

Elizabeth knelt down, and traced the etchings with her index finger. "This is absolutely incredible,"she said, breaking the silence. She looked up at me, and frowned at my obvious look of discomfort.

Something was wrong here. After the pain and discomfort experienced so far, this newly-discovered serenity left a bad taste in my mouth.

I can't say that the feeling was one of fear, but of apprehension in the extreme. Such drastic swings in luck never occur without some kind of outside impetus.

Elizabeth continued to study the markings. She was doing her best to interpret them. I squatted down next to her.

I crawled around on my hands and knees as I tried to piece together their meaning.

The chiseled magnificence of this altar was strangely familiar. Part of the scratchings were the same as those inscribed into the side of the stone I saw. I thought back, remembering when I first saw the Sun Stone. I recalled my exuberance when the piece of Sun Stone Dr. Kruger had given me fit snugly into the Sun Stone's only defect.

I was troubled that I couldn't put it all together, to come up with some explanation, not for Elizabeth, but for myself. There were too many variables to get focused.

I got up and circled the altar three or four times, studying, calculating. Like the Sun Stone I had seen, it was smooth—perfectly smooth, except for the hieroglyphics. Both were perfectly maintained. By whom?

The crystal again caught my eye. I slowly approached the altar. I reached out and touched it, dragging my finger from its base to its tip. As I did this, the crystal began to change color, melding into a deep blood red. I quickly removed my hand and turned, uneasy.

"Quickly. Elizabeth! You must see this. Quickly, quickly." I motioned to her.

She was still reading the story etched on the platform. The cavern's glow accentuated her form. She was wet from humidity and fear. She ignored me and returned to her reading.

"Something wrong?" I inquired.

Elizabeth signaled for me to be patient. Her lips mouthed words silently. She stood and came near me, a puzzled look in her face.

"According to the story, we are in a cavern called the Temple of Rajun. It is located in the Valley of the Sun, wherever that is. I'm sure this is the Temple," she said.

I sifted through my memory. I think Chawa mentioned something about this place once, but it was lost among the many other strange things he had said—or did. Certainly this piece of new information would add another piece to the puzzle, whatever the puzzle was. That was the major question, one that continued to elude me. Elizabeth interrupted my train of thought.

"This light. Where does it come from?" She was looking closely at the quartz crystal, glowing in its first color. She had barely placed her finger on its surface when, again, it began to change color, causing her to pull her hand away as if she had been burned. She said nothing. She had become entranced as I had become; Elizabeth quietly marveled at the smoothness, the simplicity of the altar.

We can't stay in here forever, I thought to myself. I need to make the most of my time. I reached in my pocket and retrieved my journal. I turned to an empty page and, with a nervous flourish, began scribbling down every single detail I could think of. I lost myself as a flood of images and feelings raced through my mind. I continued to write. I jumped at her touch and her voice.

"Let's see," she said, "how can I say this?" She paused, twisting a lock of her hair around her index finger. "Although I'm not certain, John's papers included some inscriptions that are very similar to those here. John had translated them. When I showed a special interest in them, John, with a wonderful patience, spent hours showing me their meaning. I can't decipher them all, but I do recognize a few," she admitted.

"Take a look at this one," she said, as she knelt down next to me. She carefully felt the contours of a particular set of figures. "I think this says 'This is the entrance to the hidden Kingdom of Chandi. There....'"

She paused, and shook her head and began again.

"'....Those who believe are welcome.'"

Elizabeth looked up at me. "I'm sorry," she said, "There are just too many things that I don't understand." She continued, trying to be clear through her frustration. "There are some markings I recognize, but I can't determine the context. This one here, for instance," she pointed to a symbol, "makes reference to the Sun King."

"The Sun King?" I was only half-listening to her, because there was something that she had just said that interested me.

"Those who believe are welcome?" I mumbled to myself. "What was the connection between the markings on the Sun Stone and those etched here on the alter? Was there any connection to the Stone to which Chawa had led me?"

I flipped back in my journal. I found the section I had written the day Chawa and I first reached the Sun Stone. I scanned it, reviewing some of the notes I made on the Sun Stone, and looked carefully at my primitive attempts to duplicate the symbols and scratchings.

Elizabeth sighed. "Do you recall telling me how you got that gold bracelet, that it came from someone matching the description of Chawa?" she asked. Well, I don't know if it was Chawa, or his twin brother, but what's important is that our troubles began after we met him.

"John and I, like you, were obsessed with solving the mystery of the Sun Stone, the Valley of the Sun and the Sun King. Whether or not this Chawa fellow meant to protect us, or betray us, he is the common factor. And perhaps his purpose was neither, but only to get us to believe…to believe that there really was a Sun Stone. That it wasn't legend but a very powerful reality."

"You and I drank from the waters surrounding that Stone in the lagoon yesterday, as we fled from the cannibals. Do you recall that? You weren't very lucid," I asked.

Elizabeth shook her head, clearly not remembering.

"Chawa told me that if one drinks of the water springing from around the stone, the doors of Chandi would be opened to him. But where or what is Chandi?"

We got up and carefully descended the spiral staircase to the island below.

"I don't think this is all by chance, Elizabeth," I finally said as we reached the bottom. "Out of all the places that we could have hidden last night, we picked the cave on the left. Which leads us to this place. The Temple of Rajun? And all these etchings. Too coincidental."

I went back to the stairs and sat on the first step. I again opened my journal and wrote down everything that Chawa had told me that I could remember. Elizabeth sat quietly next to me, stretching, and massaging her neck. Then she poked my ribs with her elbow.

She pointed to the ceiling of the oval room.

A thin thread of light penetrated through an opening, exactly over the altar and the protruding jag of crystal. The line of light soon appeared like a shaft of sunlight, piercing the crystal, which then diffused the light into the cavern, creating the most incredible rainbow of colors.

Elizabeth and I were mesmerized with the natural kaleidoscope. The colors emanating from the crystal were so pure and so clear. Perhaps the jag was a diamond.

Splash!! To our dismay, something—or someone—had just fallen into the pool of water. I swung my arm out, across Elizabeth, offering protection. I had the wherewithal to have brought along my pointed staff and I reached down and picked it up, ready to meet the cannibals and my doom. An eerie silence prevailed.

She pointed to the ceiling of the oval room.

A thin thread of light penetrated through an opening, exactly over the altar and the protruding jag of crystal. The line of light soon appeared like a shaft of sunlight, piercing the crystal, which then diffused the light into the cavern, creating the most incredible rainbow of colors.

My heart pounded relentlessly as I made my way toward the sound. My eyes darted back and forth, ready for an assault from either direction. I jumped as I detected movement to my left, poised, ready to defend myself.

Sitting on one of the seven stepping stones, now making his disgusting kissing noises, was my little monkey friend that had untied me in the cannibal's camp. He bared his teeth and screeched loudly, reverberating against the sides of the cavern. Then, as if his screech were a signal, a large group of his mates emerged from hiding in the recesses of the cavern. Not many seemed brave enough to venture too close, but a few of the braver ones, looking at my monkey friend for assurance, timidly approached and dropped fruit at my feet. Delicious looking fruits of every kind.

"Food!" Elizabeth and I said in unison. Without another word, we began to stuff ourselves, pausing only long enough to pick up another piece.

The monkeys continued to bring fruit, and soon we had slowed our gluttony to a more moderate degree. I looked at Elizabeth. Her face glowed golden in the light of the cavern.

CHAPTER 12

GATEWAY TO CHANDI

Elizabeth and the monkeys took an immediate liking to each other. They played with her, tumbling about for her attention. I viewed this strange interaction with much amusement...and with some jealousy, I must admit.

My monkey friend, who I now called Samo, appropriately enough, was the only one who joined my company. He was different from the others; physically as well as in manner. He had a distinctive marking right in the middle of his forehead, making him appear impish. He was mischievous; a real prankster. Three times I found my bootlaces untied. Three times to the obvious delight of Samo. He played with my holster, inserting his hand, and wiggling his fingers through the barrel end. He made strange noises, guttural in quality. He never removed his eyes from me. It was as if he didn't want to miss even a second of my experience.

Snapping to, I looked around me. We had made quite a mess of this beautiful island. Banana peels and half-finished fruit pieces dotted the area. I don't think that I would have really thought about it if it weren't for the strange behavior of Samo. Right at the top of the staircase, he carefully unfolded a large piece of fabric, coarse to the touch, and spread it out. He then began to gather together the garbage that accumulated around us.

The other monkeys, who had retired to small plateaus and cliffs that lined the caverns great walls, took notice of Samo's litter patrol. Excited screeches and chatter quickly filled my ears, as the troop of agitated monkeys jumped up and down and paced nervously to and fro. It wasn't long before all sorts of fruit and garbage rained down on us. Samo didn't stop for a moment, and continued to gather the remnants of our feast. I joined him.

We finally accumulated a pile that was quite high. He brought the four corners of the large net together, at the top of the heap, and tied them together. The garbage had now been captured, I chuckled and gave him a salute, hand to brow.

My friend dragged the garbage-filled cocoon to the edge of the moat area, and hopped out to one of the middle stones, and tossed it into the water to the right of the stones.

My hands were sticky with the juice of exotica. Elizabeth had beat me to the waters edge, on the clear side of the stones, and had knelt to wash her hands. I scurried to her side, dipping my hands in as well. A splash—Elizabeth dove into the pool, shrieking at the slap of its coldness. Not one to pass up such an opportunity, I quickly followed her. She tread water right where I broke the surface, both of us gasping for breath to ease the shock.

Again, I couldn't help notice how attractive Elizabeth was, with hair wet around her oval face. I took advantage of this brisk swim to try to douse any amorous thoughts I began to experience. I swam faster and faster, until my inner soul slowed and found its center. I floated on my back.

Something was amiss. The monkeys suddenly began a cacophony of wild screams. A funel had begun to form on the side of the pool where the ball of leftover fruit had hit the water, a pulling to the right, pivoting slowly around the exact spot of impact. Both Elizabeth and I felt the pull from our side of the pool. It slowly increased in intensity, and we slowly were pulled toward this siphon, propelled ever faster by the water spiraling down its spout. Elizabeth and I swam furiously to the edge of the pond and jumped out. Then, as if stirred and encouraged by the furious whirlpool that had began to empty this pond, a wind began to whirl about us and the monolith, adding to the din of monkey noise. The wind whipped and screamed. Elizabeth and I sought refuge next to the monolith, cowering next to the huge pillar for protection.

Abruptly, it stopped and only the occasional screech of fright broke the silence.

Samo took Elizabeth by the hand and led her to the seven stepping stones. She carefully leaped from one to the other until she reached the cavern wall.

I started to follow, but I stopped. I turned and gazed up the towering cylinder.

It was as if I was pushed. I raced up the spiral staircase and ran to the crystal. I ran my hand over it, admiring its smoothness one last time. Again it hummed to a darkening red, warning my hand. Then, to my own amazement, I pulled at the crystal. It glowed even brighter. I tried again, tugging with all my strength. I fell backwards as the crystal was freed from its anchor. It continued to glow in my hand. Spellbound, I carefully inspected this beautiful shard. It was fairly light in weight and felt good in my hand. I looked around to make sure I wasn't seen. Fortunately, the cylinder rose too high and I couldn't be seen from the cavern floor.

I hid the crystal under my shirt, whose tight weave would keep the glow dampered. I needed time. I went around to the front of the altar and placed my hands on it. I closed my eyes and promised to return the crystal. I acknowledged that I didn't know why I needed it just yet, but I knew deep in my gut that I was destined to take it. I opened my eyes, quickly descended the stairs and joined the others.

The pools had emptied. I was fascinated that so much water could be drained from this ample pond in such a short time. Why was a different matter. There was nothing left except for mud, and an occasional puddle formed by water that didn't disappear down.........down where?

The deepest part of the pond bed was right in the area where the garbage bag had sunk. Obviously, all the water had drained down this sink hole. I jumped into a foot of mud, clean mud if there can be such a thing. It had the consistency of cream, much like the mud that had covered Chawa. I slipped along to the edge of the sinkhole and peered in.

A slippery hole disappeared darkly into the belly of the earth. A strange monotone hummed ominously from deep inside the hole. I felt a pull as though something was trying to draw me down the hole—like the water. I looked down and noticed that I was now into mud up to my knees.

I tried to make my way to the bank, but was making no progress. The hum from the sinkhole got louder, and slowly the mud began to be drawn into the sinkhole.

I yelled to Elizabeth. She quickly hopped across the stones to the edge of the mud hole. Grabbing my trusted, pointed stick, she lay prone on the ground and extended the stick towards me. I was about a half meter shy of grabbing hold of it. Elizabeth eased into the mud on her belly, but not enough to reach me with the stick. Samo bounced over and held Elizabeth by the feet as she slipped into the mud just enough so I could grab the stick. That stabilized my position but made little progress from the edge of this trap. Samo screeched and was quickly joined by about ten other monkeys. Each monkey grabbed onto Elizabeth, at least what they could, and pulled her back to the island's edge, pulling me to safety as well. I extricated myself from this mire, making a loud sucking noise as I pulled my feet from the muck. Muddied, we hugged each other for the first time. I was exhausted and taking a big breath I said "Listen, Elizabeth, I have a very strong feeling that we shouldn't be here. I suggest we make our way back to the mouth of the cave. Once we're there, we can evaluate our situation. The hyenas are probably long gone by now, and hopefully the cannibals have given up and returned to their village. I think we should go back to the entrance and make our way to civilization."

With monkeys in tow, we made our way back up the path to the ledge and then around and around, this time to the right. We passed the cones of lime, still glistening, glowing. Soon, we came to the stone door that led from the cavern to the end of the tunnel. The door was closed and, at first, resisted my attempt to open it. With Elizabeth's help, we finally managed to shove it open. From there, we retraced our steps and headed down the passageway that led back to the cave's entrance. As we drew nearer, we heard a strange thing—the roar of water.

It wasn't long before we arrived at the mouth of the cave. Confusion spread across my face. I was sure we had backtracked correctly, but, strangely, a roaring waterfall now curtained the entrance, blocking our escape. I walked to the mouth of the cave. The sheet of water, thousands of liters a minute, fell steeply into......somewhere.

The monkeys seemed right at home. They hopped about the formations of slippery rock that ringed this hole behind the waterfall. I looked over the edge, shuddering at what I saw. I couldn't see through the water and I had no idea of what was on the other side. A drop of two meters......fifty meters......three hundred meters! After all, if we were back at the same spot where we had entered, well, we had climbed pretty high to get here, and I didn't remember this at all. I took a step back, rubbing my forehead as I considered the facts. I had nearly made up my mind that we might have to return to the cavern when I was joined once again by my hairy, little monkey friend, Samo. Would he bring us luck again?

He went close to the edge and looked. Up, then down. He motioned for me, and disappeared off to my right. Had he slipped? I raced to the edge, and found Samo scurrying to the next rock below with much ease, as if he had been here before.

I peered after him. I was certain that Elizabeth and I hadn't come up to the cave entrance over these huge rocks. I would have remembered that.

Nonetheless, I followed. And Elizabeth. And an army of monkeys. It wasn't too long until we had made substantial progress down the face of this sheer cliff, our progress hidden, shielded by an expanse of water that I couldn't fathom.

It became foggier and the stones became a bit slippier. But the pace never slowed. The steepness never eased. How we ever made it down I'll have to ponder some other time.

Samo stopped. A batch of orange-green flowers blossomed on a ledge above him. I remember how odd I thought that flowers should be there, hidden from the sun.

With a yelp, Samo jumped through the sheet of water, and disappeared to whatever the other side offered. I hesitated. Several of the monkeys pushed me to the side and, in turn, each jumped into the pounding waterfall. The rush was fierce once those first monkeys made the leap. I called to Elizabeth, trying to reach her only to be hindered by the onslaught of monkeys.

She soon stumbled toward me. Without breaking stride, we both jumped from the ledge as far as we could.

We landed hard. On dry ground. A surprise, believe me, that the drop was only two meters. My back throbbed, having landed awkwardly.

Elizabeth cried with pain, grabbing at her knee, the very one she had problems with earlier. I took account of my other limbs, checking for cuts—checking reality.

I managed to stand, and walked a few feet behind a gathering of monkeys, who stood chattering, pointing. I looked up. Before me was the most beautiful landscape I had ever imagined. This can't be happening. This wasn't even remotely like the place where Elizabeth and I first took shelter under that big pile of rocks, below the cave's entrance.

I didn't know for sure where we were. But I suspected that we had just gone through the door to **CHANDI.**

CHAPTER 13

THE ARRIVAL

The most beautiful place I had ever seen during my time on earth shimmered before me. I rubbed my eyes, and half-expected it to disappear when I refocused. Yet it remained: a valley arrayed in greens, light, dark and emerald, softened by a wash of soft golden light. Nearby, a lagoon, still and deep blue, a mirror reflecting the sky above. Every species of ferns and grasses swayed in rhythm to the dry breeze, occasionally touching the water to enjoy its coolness. Protecting these smaller plants were some of the tallest trees I had ever seen, whose branches also bent with the breeze, waving hello to the sun. Flamingos waded quietly at one end of the lagoon, stopping often to peck at the water to retrieve some morsel seen only by them. Their beautiful colors offered a stunning contrast to the dominating green shades.

This stunning beauty was such a shock that I was totally oblivious to the fact that I was soaking wet, my clothes drenched from my leap of faith through the waterfall. I surveyed my surroundings, determined to make sense of what just happened.

I was puzzled because the cave mouth that was up this cliff had to be the one that Elizabeth and I had used in our escape from the cannibals and hyenas. I knew for sure because we had to remove more rocks from the barrier we had built to reach the waterfall.

I turned to look up the cliff. The water rushed constantly over a spill about 65 meters above this dry ground I stood on. I estimated that the mouth of the cave was about 39 meters up the cliff.

I looked around me and then back up to the cave mouth. I backtracked a bit, climbing a few wet rocks, and lifted my head to see how far we had descended. I couldn't see because there was so much water.

This was not the land Elizabeth and I left when we clawed our way up the hill to avoid the bite of either hyena or cannibal. It was a short hill and we reached it quickly, I remembered, reliving those terror-filled moments. And the waterfall?

To confuse me further, the only familiar sight was the pile of rocks behind which we first hid from the hyenas. It was over to my right, at the base of a grassy hump.

Our leap through the waterfall had left us on a rise that overlooked a vast valley. I allowed my eyes to slowly sweep the landscape, taking in all I could. The valley was like an island, nestled secretly in a ring of rock and dirt that rose abruptly from all sides of the valley, perhaps the inner walls of an ancient crater. I quickly filed through the recesses of my memory, trying to recall anything that I had heard or studied. I vaguely remembered the mention of a "valley that lay in the crater of Tan" in a parchment fragment Dr. Kruger had given me, but because it was mentioned only once, I disregarded it as mere legend.

I decided to mention this to Elizabeth, hoping that she, too, had come across anything like this during her studies with John. I walked over to her side, joining her as she scanned the fabulous land that lay before her.

I whispered in her ear, "Have you ever heard of the Crater of Tan?"

"Tan?" She walked away from me and headed toward the lagoon, her mind elsewhere. Perhaps she, too, was confused about our whereabouts.

For now, our surroundings seemed safe. I felt reasonably sure that our trouble with the cannibals was a thing of the past. It wouldn't be excised from my memory for a long time, but, for the moment, I relaxed.

I found a shady spot a few feet from the lagoon, and propped myself against a tree. The breeze licked at my face. I reached into my pants pocket and removed my tattered journal. I opened it to the first available blank page and began to write. I recalled the events of the past day and wrote a detailed account of the experience in the cavern and tried to be as descriptive as I could about its appearance. Time slipped away, and as I began to jot down my immediate impressions of this newfound valley, I was distracted by the sound of someone plunging into the lagoon.

I looked up to see a laughing, re-energized Elizabeth bobbing in the water, disappearing for a few moments only to break its surface some distance from where she had gone underwater. A dozen or so of our monkey friends cavorted happily in the trees and in the water, playing games.

I returned to my journal, now partially darkened by the shadows creeping over the pages. I continued to write and, to the best of my ability, sketch some drawings of the caverns, the underground altar, and the panorama of the valley. I attempted to draw some maps, from my memory. I don't know how accurate they were, but it really didn't matter. Who knew if we would ever find our way back here…if we ever found our way out.

I raised my head and rocked it back and forth, rolling it about my shoulders, stretching the muscles on each side. As I rolled my head to one side, a shiny reflection at the other end of the valley caught my eye. It disappeared behind the foliage of the trees, but twinkled sporadically as the swaying branches passed between it and my line of vision.

I got up and stared intently in the direction of the sparkle. I made my way back up to the rise were we had jumped through the waterfall. I put my hand above my eyes to create shade for them, and squinted inquisitively at the area where the reflection had first peeked out.

There it was again, but it was too far away. Whatever it was, the light that reflected off of it was blinding, making it impossible to determine what it was. I first considered possible danger. Perhaps more cannibals, a thought that caused a painful knot deep in my gut. I quickly returned to the lagoon to fetch Elizabeth and to find a safe hiding place, a refuge in which we could be safe until I determined what threat prevailed.

I found Elizabeth languishing under a tree near my writing spot, lying alluringly on a mat of palm fronds that had been fashioned by the monkeys. Her eyes were closed, and her chest heaved with deep breathing. I called to her, but she either didn't hear me, or was just ignoring me, content to be quietly resting.

When twilight finally arrives, I thought, maybe I will be able to determine what caused the bright reflection. I had come to learn that anything might bring danger and I wasn't enthusiastic about facing new episodes any time soon.

My exhaustion soon overwhelmed my fears. I found my resting spot and settled again against the trunk of the tree.

I sat quietly, breathing in the beauty of my surroundings. The bluest sky imaginable, streaked with wisps of clouds, caused my spirit to soar. I closed my eyes and imagined I was in Eden. Momentarily, danger and negative thoughts evaporated, seeming unimportant. Whatever problems lurked nearby, they would have to wait. I weaved in and out of consciousness—contentment flooded my body. Suddenly I realized that everything around me had become eerily quiet.

Our monkey friends had ceased their chatter—I pricked my ears for danger.

I opened my eyes and found myself face to face with a muscular, sleek leopard. It sat on its haunches, watching me closely. My natural reaction to reach slowly for my gun was replaced by the sorry reality that I had no gun.

Seconds, minutes ticked off the clock. It seemed a lifetime that the leopard and I were frozen in each other's sight. Finally, and ever so slowly, the huge cat began to move towards me. The hollowness in the pit of my stomach deepened as he closed the distance between us. I couldn't move a single muscle and my breathing caught in my throat.

He finally reached me and we were practically nose to nose. With his eyes steady on mine, his cold nose touched my nose. He then began to sniff me curiously. I dared not even blink my eyes.

He moved around me, sniffing about the ground, and then disappeared behind me, out of my line of sight. I stiffened and prepared myself for a vicious rear attack. Fear frothed in my mouth, and the pain in my lungs grew the longer I held my breath. After a brief period of time, my breathing returned to normal, although I still stared straight ahead, contemplating my next move. I had to do something, so I slowly turned and looked behind me. Nothing. The leopard had gone its own way. A huge sense of relief surged through my body.

As I was trying to decide if I had been dreaming—confronting a figment of a very tired mind—or if what I had seen was real, my thoughts were broken by the sound of human voices—voices brought to my ears by the wind.

The voices were still distant, but the prevailing breeze brought forewarning. I tried to determine their origin.

I scrambled again to the rise above the valley, in front of the waterfall, cautiously hiding among the rocks and foliage. I surveyed the valley, paying particular attention to the direction from which the voices seemed to come. Several kilometers away, the movement of a group of people caught my eye. From here, I couldn't determine if they were natives, although some looked as if they had very dark skin. They weren't naked, and their clothes and jewelry reflected the sun. I watched closely. In the midst of this group, there was an individual who appeared to be special. From what I could tell, his skin was tattooed like that of a leopard. Perhaps he was a king of sorts, or a priest. He was clothed in bright colors and adorned in gold.

Then a strange thing happened. While I know that he couldn't have seen me, being so far away and unaware of my presence, he looked my direction and, uncannily, seemed to lock his eyes on mine. For a few brief seconds, I thought he was Chawa.

Then he looked away, saying something to the man on his left. The casual nature of this entourage made me think that they were out for an afternoon stroll, enjoying their surroundings, and chatting among themselves, unaware of our presence.

Suddenly, the sound of a powerful gong filled the valley. Three strikes in succession. The depth of pitch of this sound, and the length of time it took to swell to its full volume bespoke of its huge size. The final blow resonated for at least a minute, filling the valley with a shimmering tone that waned slowly and evenly.

I watched the band of natives carefully. They stopped, and as if nothing extraordinary had happen, turned and retraced their steps, perhaps returning to the place from where they had come. My eyes followed them intently, occasionally losing them among the rocks and vegetation, but quickly relocked on them when they emerged from their natural cover.

I slipped down the slope, scraping my knee. I headed towards Elizabeth and was surprised that she still lay motionless, dozing gently in the shade of the tall palm tree.

Hadn't she been roused by the distant sound of the gong? Hadn't she heard the voices?

Seeing her sleeping so soundly caused me to yawn, to become conscious of my own exhaustion. I'm tired, too, Elizabeth, I mused, but you don't see me drifting off into nowhere land. I then thought of my slip in and out of twilight earlier, embarrassed at my selfish thinking. I decided to let her sleep and found my way back to my resting tree. I sat down heavily, frightening a brown frog who was sunning on a nearby lilypad. It jumped to safety and swam to the middle of the lagoon. I watched it closely, wishing that we could reach safety as easily as he had.

Again, I rolled my head about my neck, stretching the sinews to their limit. I looked over to where Elizabeth lay, and found my view obstructed by a pair of strong and completely muddied legs. Startled, I looked up, expecting to find a cannibal greedily licking his lips.

"Chawa!" I blurted.

I was overcome with emotion—emotion mixed with anger and happiness.

I stood and was promptly met by his extended hand, something he had never done before. In his characteristic way, he stared intently into my eyes, and then allowed a broad grin to spread across his face.

"Welcome to Chandi!" he said.

He took my hand and squeezed it, not a shake but a serious grip. He continued to look at me, never allowing his eyes to wander from mine.

I wasn't sure how to respond. I battled my feelings. Questions raced through my mind. What happened to you? Why did you desert me? Did you know the cannibals captured me? Do you know Elizabeth? How did you know I was here? Have you been following us?.... I didn't know where to begin.

He nodded his head toward the still sleeping Elizabeth. "Wake her up. The gong has already sounded and we are expected."

"Now just a bloody minute," I protested. "Who's expecting us? Where are we and where do we need to go? If you had any idea what I've been through the past......."

Chawa looked at me, then walked over to Elizabeth. He shook her lightly and she mumbled incoherently as she broke free from her slumber.

When Elizabeth's eyes finally focused on Chawa, she showed no fear. She looked at me, then back at Chawa.

He offered his hand, and she used it to pull herself to her feet.

She brushed off and then held up her hand. "This is the man that gave me the golden rope bracelet."

I immediately looked down to my wrist, making sure that I still had mine.

"Is this Chawa, Alan"? she asked.

I nodded yes and walked towards them.

"Quickly. Waste no time in following me," he whispered.

Chawa brushed by me in his familiar gait. I took Elizabeth's hand and we followed.

CHAPTER 14

THE PALACE GUEST

It wasn't long before I noticed that our monkey friends, who had been chattering and playing among the trees as we followed Chawa, had disappeared. I couldn't hear them anymore, and couldn't see any either. Both Elizabeth and I breathed a simultaneous sigh. We looked at each other and, though not a word was spoken, the air was steeped in apprehension.

We had been walking about a half hour when the sound of drumming and music tickled my ears. It got louder and louder. Then, across a stretch of meadow, there rose out of the ground the most magnificent palace I had ever seen, the sun reflecting brilliantly off a green copper dome that rose high into the sky.

I looked over at Elizabeth and then back to the palace standing before me. I saw no people, but we were still several hundred meters away.

An impatient Chawa turned to us.

"Come," he commanded. He seemed at ease, as if he had arrived home. He confidently led us across the meadow to a pool at the bottom of a sweeping staircase, fed with water from a golden trough that divided the grand

We went up a few steps and through a fabulous archway supported by two magnificent stone carved pillars and into an expansive portico that was no less extraordinary than all that I had seen up to now.

staircase. He continued past the pool and staircase and followed a pathway that took a circuitous route, through more jungle foliage, to a terraced area with a fountain in its middle, just outside the palace. It was from here that the water flowed into the golden trough to feed the pool below. To our right, the rest of the palace stretched out before us. There appeared to be several terraces jutting from its side, abutting the sides of a sparkling pool.

Chawa continued and motioned for us to follow. We went up a few steps and through a fabulous archway supported by two magnificent stone carved pillars and into an expansive portico that was no less extraordinary than all that I had seen up to now. In the middle of the round room was a solid bronze sculpture of a life-size elephant.

"This is the Elephant Wing of the Palace. You will see many sculpted animals throughout the palace," Chawa told us. Elizabeth and I surveyed the room, its grandeur quite breathtaking. "Wait here and I'll escort Elizabeth to the princess' wing."

I was so overcome by the beauty and artistry of this magnificent place that, though I heard his voice, it didn't register what he had said, and I didn't notice when he and Elizabeth left.

The magnificence of this castle spread out before me.

"Not a scratch. Not a scuff," I mumbled. I looked up, trying to find signs of life. There wasn't a soul in sight.

Burning torches were everywhere, and the glow accentuated the luster of the floor.

"Chawa. Who owns this place? Who lives here?" I asked as I straightened. He didn't answer. I turned to my left and repeated my inquiry. "Are you going to answ.....?"

I quickly looked to my right and again to my left and was startled to find myself alone. There was no Chawa. There was no Elizabeth. It then occurred to me that I had not seen other inhabitants of the palace, and except for the hum of the rainforest, the palace stood muted.

I stood confused for a moment, trying to make sense of my situation. Chawa and Elizabeth had disappeared and I hadn't heard a sound. I saw no others. I was alone.

As far as I could tell, I stood alone at the east end of the huge palace. To my left, openings in the wall allowed the noise of the surrounding rainforest to enter and resonate. Certain that Elizabeth and Chawa didn't go over the wall, I walked around the huge elephant sculpture until I stood at the entrance of a hall, one so long I couldn't see the other end. I did see movement, though, and someone, a figure as small as a speck, got larger and larger as the distance between us diminished.

He was a middle aged man with a big smile—a man that obviously was trained in the art of being a host. He was about my height and trim in build. Like Chawa, and Elizabeth and myself for that matter, he wore the same golden bracelet on his wrist. His was different, though, because two silver icons were woven into the fibrous ends of the bracelet. Mine and the others' just hung loose, frayed.

I didn't dare move. Without thinking, more out of habit, I think, I straightened myself, and smoothed my soiled clothes the best I could, wanting to make a good impression. His footfalls echoed with a clop down the spacious corridor, which was so long, that it took almost three minutes for this oncoming stranger to reach the Hall of Elephants, as Chawa called it.

The stranger extended his hand and his smile put my fears to rest. "Mr. Bunt, I am Inzer, and I am at your service. It is my purpose to make your stay here pleasant," he said reassuring me with a big, friendly smile.

Out of courtesy, I shook his hand, while I blurted, "How did you know my name? What happened to the woman that was with me a few moments ago?"

Inzer held up his hand, and shook his head knowingly. "Mr. Bunt, you have my promise that no harm will come to the woman. She has been escorted to the Princess' wing. That is all I can tell you. Soon, I'm sure many of your questions will be answered. But for now, I must insist that you believe me and cooperate to your fullest ability. Please. Won't you follow me?"

Inzer made an about-face and began to retrace his earlier steps. Having little choice, I followed close behind.

It's difficult to describe this place. In all of my travels, I have never seen a structure so magnificent. The attention to every detail was extraordinary. Its intricate craftsmanship was at least as refined, if not surpassing that I had seen in Florence and Rome.

Inzer allowed me to tarry; he must have recognized my awe of this place.

"We are very proud of our palace," he offered.

I could only shake my head in disbelief. This place must have taken years to design and build.

Finally, having enough of tiptoeing around the hard questions, I looked over at

Inzer. "I don't understand," I complained. "We have been brought here by a gentleman known as Chawa. Do you know of such a man?"

"Ah, yes, Chawa." Inzer stopped. He then looked up at me, and with a sense of urgency, saying, "I must show you to your quarters. It is important that you get some rest, and perhaps take a meal, if you desire. Tomorrow is a long day.... Come."

He went about twenty paces and turned to his left down another corridor, this one not quite as long. The hue of the color washing in this hallway was a shade of blue, as the oil lamps that showed the way flickered with the strangest blue flame. We bore a bit to our right and proceeded across a portico constructed with white elephant tusks. I stopped.

"Come, Mr. Bunt. I must show you to your room with no further delays. When we get you settled, I will be happy to answer your questions."

My room was comfortable. I must say that it was pretty plain compared with the intricacy and workmanship of the rest of the Palace. The room was furnished with a table, a few chairs, and a single bed against one wall, opposite an opening that went out to a balcony.

"I hope you will find this satisfactory during your stay here. Everything you need or require will be provided," offered Inzer.

In the middle of the table was a large woven box that contained fruits.

"You know, Mr. Inzer, I am too confused and have too many questions to eat right now. Certainly sleep is out of the question. I would appreciate it if you would join me on the balcony and tell me what I want to know. Can you do that?" I politely said. "I mean, my companion has disappeared and I don't know where she is. I'm not quite certain even where I am." Inzer said, "Yes, I suppose you deserve some answers. At least I can shed a bit of light on your situation." He moved to the balcony and sat in a leather chair and bid me to take the one opposite him. Fruit and fresh water were on the table beside my chair, but I ignored them as my hunger had faded.

CHAPTER 15

"THE LEGEND" YEAR 492

After settling in our chairs, we both enjoyed a moment of quiet reflection. Inzer began. "The reasons for your being here I am not fully sure, and I never have met someone like you. Your dress is strange and I have no idea from where you have come, but I have been instructed by someone very important and highly respected to see that you have everything you need for your comfort and peace of mind. It is my understanding that you are special and I am to answer your questions to the best of my ability."

"I appreciate that, for I do have many, many questions. One, I have no idea where I am and why we have been brought to this place. My companion has been separated from me and I am quite concerned about her safety." I tried to be as calm yet as forceful as I could without being threatening.

Inzer nodded his head, probably evaluating my mood and my obvious apprehension. "What I am about to tell you will seem unbelievable and difficult to comprehend in your present situation, but you must remember, this is the Kingdom of Chandi. Kindly bear with me as I tell you of an ancient legend, one I think will enlighten you about things in which my people believe. The events which you are about to hear happened many centuries ago. So please listen carefully. As it was revealed to me, I will tell it to you now. Long ago, there was a great King, who ruled the most powerful empire of those days. Its beauty, wealth and power was known to the four corners of the world and the mere mention of the King's name made his enemies tremble in awe. His friends were proud to be considered as such to this conqueror. He was a legend in his own time.

"The legend says that, as was tradition in this Kingdom, this King ascended to the throne on his thirty-ninth birthday. His father, the King whom he was replacing, presented him with a gift of four beautiful maidens to be his lawful wives. They had been specially chosen and each was brought from a different cardinal point in the world. Naturally, each had impeccable lineage. All of them were deeply honored and had quickly agreed to marry this King. The festivities lasted a good part of that entire year. Highly esteemed dignitaries and friends participated in the betrothal celebrations.

"The festivities finally ended when each of the four brides were found to be with child. Immediately, preparations began so the first-born son could be received royally, as this circumstance required. Since no one knew which princess would produce the first-born and the rightful heir to the throne, it became something of a game of speculation as to who would give birth first. In all of this Kingdom's history, this had not happened before. The old ones said it was written in the stars and the only thing to do was wait without worry.

"As fate would have it, exactly two hundred and seventy-five days after the wedding date, each of the four princesses gave birth to perfectly healthy boys all on the same day! As there was no precedent for this, all four babies were recognized as first-born, each with an undeniable right of succession to the throne.

"Foreseeing the possibility of this happenstance, the new King, together with the councilmen and the high priests (following the advice of Mur, the most powerful of the magicians ever to live in this land), agreed to observe the oldest law known to them. This elite group decided to proclaim a new edict, which they engraved into an awesome chunk of jade. In this edict, they told of the Kingdom, the history of its people, its beliefs and of its contributions to civilization. For many years this stone was displayed in the most prominent place of the city, accessible to everyone, so all could admire and learn from it. News about this stone reached the farthest reaches of the world. Eventually, a name was given to it: 'The Sun Stone'.

"Significantly mentioned on The Sun Stone was the day that the four sons would celebrate their thirteenth birthday. When that day finally arrived, the people were summoned to participate in a unique ceremony. As the sky painted itself blue and the soft morning light illuminated The Sun Stone in all its splendor, the King's strong voice declared: 'These are my four beloved sons whose blood ordains them successors to my empire.'

"The proud King then proceeded to place each son's back against The Sun Stone, each facing the cardinal point from where his mother had come almost fourteen years earlier. Next, he commanded them to walk exactly thirteen steps from the Sun Stone. Once the sons paced off thirteen steps, the King approached the stone, invoked several strange sayings and incantations, and, with all of his strength, threw The Sun Stone from its pedestal. Anguish and astonishment surged through the gathering. A few shook their heads in agreement, realizing that the King's actions had been agreed thirteen years before. As such, these few weren't surprised when The Sun Stone separated in exactly four equal pieces but rather, rejoiced! The

King then commanded each son to claim, as his own, the piece of the Stone that had crashed nearest to him. Each piece was a symbol of his share of the empire.

"Then the King said to the gathering: 'Not even my beloved sons, these princes, are worthy of becoming Kings just because they were born sons to a King. Each man in this Kingdom proves his worth by fighting for the position he wants in life; even more so, I expect this from my own sons, each of whose merits I know well. Therefore, each of you shall have to strive for perfection on your own. For how else can you consider yourselves worthy of ruling over the most important empire ever to have existed until you learn the profound knowledge needed to develop undying loyalty to your heritage and the wisdom to act justly and with infinite compassion towards our people? You also must remember that the unity among you is the key to your new empire. For, you see, if I take a single stick in my hand and bend it, it breaks easily. But if I hold four sticks tightly together and try to break them, it is impossible. Remember, strength and invincibility will exist if there is a strong union among you.'

"The very next day was Spring's first day, cause for another celebration in the Kingdom. As in every year, the time for great displays of beauty and happiness had arrived. The harmonious voices of all the gleeful inhabitants, their sweet melodies dancing in the wind, lulled the valley, only giving way to the excited drums, pleading to Mother Earth that she continue with her generosity and bountifulness one more season. Usually this was a not solemn occasion, but this year the festivities were overshadowed by the ceremonial farewell.

"On the second day of the celebration, the monarch paired each son with the High Priest who had been watching over him since the day he had been born. The King also presented each son with a special piece of cloth—one specifically woven by each of their mothers—in which to wrap his particular piece of the jade Sun Stone, since his piece of stone represented the key to his own future and, more importantly, his right to rule. The King then asked four thousand strong men, the bravest in the land, if they were willing to follow their Prince to the end of the known world. Four thousand answered they would.

"The King then spoke these farewell words: 'My beloved sons, you are now to start your own personal journey; one every man has to do for himself. Deep in your heart, you know already that you can rely on your own drum, creating a rhythm that belongs only to you. Don't allow fear to give you pause—just follow your drums rhythm. As you make your journey, look for all things that are positive. Be ready to learn all that is worth learning from every man, tribe or land you may

THE FOUR TRIBES EXODUS

encounter. Share all the good you carry with you and all that could be of any help to them. You soon will learn there is more happiness in giving than in receiving. Do not be concerned with when you must end your journey or when you will reunite with your brothers. Time is a knowing teacher and it will guide you home when the proper moment arises. **"The King raised his arms and intoned these words:** ***'When you finally find the Valley that lies in the Crater of Tan, in the Grand Oasis, where the kudu, the leopard and the crane live in harmony and the sun's shadow lies to the south, you will have finally found Chandi—your Kingdom.'*** **The King looked down at his four sons and said,** ***'Remember, only those of you who carry the stone can claim the Kingdom.'***

"The celebration continued for three days. The air was filled with chants of longing and mystery. At night, Magician's Mur's tricks would illuminate the skies, a pale imitation of the promised glory the future would bring.

"Just before dawn on the fourth day, the King's four sons started their journey, each to the land from where their mothers had come, each following his heart's desire and determined to learn all about that which their father had spoken. Each son disappeared over the horizon to the adventure that awaited them.

"So it came to be that each prince, in his quest, crossed strange lands and raging seas. Each prince soon found a woman, one willing and eager to join him in their journey. Each marriage produced beautiful babies, some blonde and rosy, others of darker skin color, depending on the mother's coloring. All had the same luminous dark eyes of their princely father—the same dark eyes each prince inherited from their father, the Sun King.

"The prince who headed North was named 'Shukan'. He reached the farthest of the existing northern highlands and began in earnest the study of the oldest of the sciences: astronomy. Prince Shukan, under the guidance of his guardian High Priest, learned, by studying carefully the movements of the heavenly bodies, the many useful benefits of measuring the length of the day. He learned to time, predict eclipses, and understand the tides. Shukan's followers began to believe that the movements of the stars revealed the future. Shukan and his tribe became powerful and important people everywhere they went. For many years, they traveled extensively around the Northern Isles in their quest for more knowledge. Shukan's contribution to the science of astronomy was of great importance, and is known far and wide even today.

"The Prince who headed South was named 'Shaksen'. He and his people found civilizations advanced in knowledge about medicine and magic. This was a blessing since this Prince possessed the kind of mind required of a good medicine man. Shaksen not only learned how to heal, but became quite knowledgeable about natural remedies—those culled from medicinal plants, roots, and seeds. He learned the value of chants and the soothing bathes that were very popular in these regions. Naturally, Shaksen also learned how to recognize, plant and grow medicinal plants, something he planned to do when he finally arrived to Chandi. Shaksen and his tribe's fame preceded them everywhere they went. The Prince's ability to heal became legend.

"The third Prince, 'Shanktul,' headed East. He and his followers visited lands and people that were quite different in skin and eye color. Their religious beliefs were like a woven tapestry of rites, traditions and mystic symbols. This greatly interested Shanktul, who eventually learned to accept a life steeped in time-honored, yet unsatisfying traditions. Shanktul's tribe searched endlessly for deep understanding of things spiritual, but always seemed to fall short in being satisfied with what they learned or discovered in their quest. When time bid Shanktul and his tribe to return to Chandi, they did so, but the insatiable thirst for spiritual knowledge and enlightenment was to shadow this Prince and his tribe forever.

"The fourth Prince was named 'Sholksun.' He and his tribe headed West, not allowing even the Big Sea to keep them from their quest. Sholksun was sure he and his tribe would find what they were after. This tribe found diversity in climate, the people and in their ways of life. It was another world, replete with strange dwelling and customs.

"Sholksun's tribe became a practical and hardworking tribe. They learned the art of building and design. They became artists and craftsmen who elevated the act of construction to a science. Their contribution to the places they visited were the beautiful buildings they left behind on their journey. This tribe traveled the farthest and they were gone a very long time.

"No account is given as to how long each prince's quest was. Neither do we know if the four princes ever communicated among themselves, or if they ever crossed paths with one another. We only know that at the beginning of a New Year, the four Princes and their tribes, now much larger than when they began, reunited.

The first ones to arrive were the northern tribe. The tribe of Shukan-tan. They came through the ridge and following the strict orders issued by the High Priest, Prince Shukan crossed the cavern and upon the presentation of his piece of The Sun Stone, found himself and his tribe welcomed into the Great Valley and the Oasis of Chandi, their final destiny, as the prophecy had said.

Soon after, the tribe coming from the Southlands arrived carrying a numerous variety of plants and seeds, some never seen before. After the Prince's presentation of his part of the stone, they received their welcome too. They too rejoiced in the happiness of having found a place to call home at last.

The East bound tribe, the tribe of Shanktul-tan, followed their enlightened Prince Shanktul, who carried the third piece of stone. Serenity and contentment filled them as they arrived – a feeling that spread through all the other new inhabitants of the valley, even as they continued waiting.

Just three moons later the last of the Princes and his tribe known as the Sholksun-tan, arrived from their long journey from the West. Upon the presentation of the last missing stone, the superb piece now rested on an altar especially made for the occasion, while wonderful things started to happen in the cavern. It was placed in its designated place of honor, the exact center of the Kingdom, as was fit for such a valuable possession, and where the people of the valley could pay homage. However, the moment the collocation ceremony had officially ended and the people were beginning to disperse, a heavy rainfall started quite unexpectedly and for thirteen days did not stop. Soon a lagoon surrounded the stone; they named it Chandi's Lagoon, since the people considered it a special gift from the heavens, as proof of a job well done. Each Prince Shukan, Shaksen, Shanktul, and Sholksun had fulfilled the expected role and proven his noble heritage.

For the entire thirteen days of continuous rain, the great council discussed the matter of succession. On the last day a decision was made: the Princes would speak for themselves.

The astronomy oriented Prince's main interest was only to ask permission to build a great observatory, like the ones that existed up in Northern Greenland's, a venerable place where he could continue his studies and observations in relation to the unending mysterious skies and its stars. Shukan was willing to swear loyalty to his new King, which ever brother that was (or were if in the plural,) even abdicate his share of the land and riches in exchange for the absolute liberty to dedicate himself solely to his passion, the studies of the skies. He truly believed he and his people would be of great service to the Kingdom's welfare, since he thought that he who rules and conquers other nations has no greater value than he who can persuade the earth to be bountiful and so feed his people abundantly. He was absolutely sure that with their applied knowledge over how to control the tides, and the time for crops, together with his mastery of measuring the length of a day, they at the end would be far more valuable to the empire and to its King.

The Southbound Prince Shaksen and his people, truly scientific and physically oriented, since their arrival had dedicated heart and soul to the physical care of the inhabitants of the valley, with all their acquired knowledge and new medical skills. Naturally the farthest thing from this Prince's mind was to rule such a vast Kingdom. Instead, he expressed his desire to build a place totally dedicated to the well being of every inhabitant that may unfortunately need their services, a rehabilitation center. He needed a special place, an extension of land to grow the huge variety of medicinal plants they had brought back with so much effort. He was eager to swear loyalty to his new King, in his name and in behalf of his tribe. Shaksen expressed his belief in a phrase: "There is no greater Kingdom or more powerful, than one that has conquered the worst of all of man's enemies: disease"

Next spoke Prince Shanktul returning from the East, leader of the philosophical tribe. Once they arrived and celebrated in happiness with the Valley, they had retired to the highest ridge, from where they contemplated the magnificent view, yet they had retired from the natural coming and going of the inhabitants' daily noisy activities. They welcomed the seclusion and quietness in order to continue listening to their inner voices. They knew how and were willing to teach all those who felt the need or wanted to learn about the many ways a man can learn to live in peace and harmony, not only with his neighbor, but most importantly, with himself. Prince Shanktul on behalf of the tribe expressed their feelings of loyalty to their new King and graciously offered themselves to write and preserve to the best of their ability the old writings for the sake of posterity.

The last to speak was the Prince Sholksun coming from the West. He was peace-loving, respectful of his traditions and committed strongly in his belief and love for his people. In the clearness of his mind, he knew he was the chosen one. So he asked for his brothers' acknowledgment and blessings. He waited for the High Priests' investment and the acceptance words, and they soon said:

"Hail to you, who has proven to be of noble heritage and worthy lineage, whose justice shall prevail at all times, and whose sword will destroy the evil and the wicked, shall they come to our walls; never in our land shall we see the strong oppress the weak. On your life and with your blood you must swear to rule not only over your own people, but all of those who may one day come to live under your law. So vast your empire shall be, that from this valley to where the sun shines upon a walking man's shoulders for three hundred and sixty-five days, all men shall know your name and live under your rule. From now on, Sholksun, the title of Sun King, is now yours forever."

The new Crown King swore and promised to live not only to fulfill his oath, but to erect in this crater of Tan, where the Oasis of Chandi existed, the most beautiful city ever conceived in any human mind before. With the mixture of styles and the knowledge brought from the North, South, East and West. The legendary Lost City in The Valley of the Sun was born under the inspiration of a monarch everyone named: **Sun King.**

When the magnificent city was completed, it truly resembled none other known to man in those days. Indeed the Palace's magnitude seemed to occupy the entire valley, including in its gardens all of the impressive waterfalls and their reflecting lagoons that were like serene mirrors during the day. By night, when it was illuminated by hundreds of torches, it was nearly impossible to decide where the real palace began and where it ended, since its dancing reflection in the water that surrounded it made it look like a mirage.

Then followed a time to remember, as it was so well described with anticipation in The Sun Stone for the generations and posterity.

"It was a fantasy Kingdom, beautiful and inhabited only by good people, where love and respect prevailed among them. They had learned and developed strong beliefs, so necessary for man's spiritual needs. Not only as a doctrine but in the sincere daily exercise of good deeds towards its fellowmen."

The transformation brought an important change in the history of this civilization and all the new lands that were later conquered. Above all, that first Sun King gave its Kingdom and the people of his time a peaceful place that allowed them to prosper.

Inzer sat back and eyed me carefully, probably trying to determine if I had been paying attention. "Well, Mr. Bunt," Inzer said, "that is our ancient legend. Tomorrow is the Celebration of Chandi. There, you will meet our Sun King and his four daughters. I have much more to tell you. But until then, you must rest. I'll return early in the morning."

Inzer excused himself and I was left alone. I knew that I would fall asleep in my chair if I did not move to the bed. I got up, went to the edge of the bed and began to remove my clothing. As I undid my shirt, the crystal fell out onto the bed covers. I had completely forgotten about it, but quickly snatched it up, hid it close to me, and suspiciously looked around to see if anyone had seen. I decided to hide the crystal, for now, behind a candle flickering from an inset in the wall. It wasn't visible from there, and I walked to several points in the room to make sure.

Comfortable that it was safe, I finished removing my clothes and laid them across the chair at the foot of the bed. I sat down and I wrote in my journal: 'Here

I find myself in a time-honored land full of enchantment that has easily dazzled me. It is a Kingdom that could only be conceived in a dream. The extraordinary palace is surrounded by crystal-clear lagoons that reflect the immense beauty of this good land and its harmony. Since my arrival, I have been treated with respect and dignity, although seeing Elizabeth would lift my heart. I am concerned, however, that something is not quite right; that this place is not a part of the African continent of 1895 we left thirteen days ago when Elizabeth and I entered the cavern. Perhaps we left time as we know it—maybe we are dead and just don't know it.'

After writing this, I went to the bed and laid down. I was asleep before my head hit the pillow.

CHAPTER 16

FESTIVITIES

Still dark, I was awakened very early to the sound of children, happily screeching and chattering. I stretched as I walked to the balcony, eager to investigate the noise, as I had seen no one except Inzer since I had arrived at the Palace.

I was quite surprised at what I saw as I peered over the edge of the balcony. The scene was filled with torches and bright, flashy colors and there was an air of excitement and festivities. The cries of delight and laughter were contagious and I decided I might as well join in the merriment.

I turned and walked back into my room, surprised to find my clothes cleaned and neatly folded at the foot of my bed. Great service, I thought. But finding them there gave me pause and I anxiously looked toward the place where I had hidden the crystal. I strode over and reached behind the candle and to my relief, it was still there. I pulled out the crystal, and for a moment, found myself entranced by its perfection and beauty. I held it tightly in my hand.

As I got dressed, my mind drifted to Elizabeth and her safety. Inzer had assured me that she was safe and, after experiencing his hospitality last evening, I had no reason to doubt him. As a matter of fact, I felt very confident that she was okay and decided to wait and see what this day brought. Perhaps I would see her.

A knock on the door brought me out of my daydream. I quickly finished buttoning my shirt, and stuffed the crystal inside, securing it in the waist of my pants. I went to the door and opened it to be greeted by an exquisitely dressed Inzer, who apologized for his intrusion. He was followed by several sparsely dressed young women, who had brought food and drink for me.

I commented on the excitement and unusual activity that appeared to be going on in the palace. Inzer made his way across the room and out to the balcony again. The women followed him, and after they had finished laying out the fruits and nuts before us, took their leave. Inzer called to me to join him and I settled into my chair.

"What's going on out there?" I asked Inzer.

"Today is the beginning of the Celebration of the Sun Stone" he began. "It is an event that has been enjoyed by all inhabitants of the Kingdom since the return of the four sons of the very first Sun King. It is a festival that celebrates the reunification of the Sun Stone; when the final quarter was restored to make it whole and, therefore, make Chandi whole."

"Ah, yes. We had finished with their story last night. It seems that you were going to tell me about the King and his four daughters. Am I to meet them?" I asked hopefully.

Inzer's eyes narrowed. "In good time, my kind sir. You will meet them during the celebration, but before then, I think it is important for you to know their significance for us."

"Please, tell me more about the Sun King, if you would be so kind," I encouraged.

"Gladly" he said. "I am sure that as soon you meet the King this would be your assessment."

THE SUN KING

Inzer paused for a moment, appearing to gather together his thoughts. He looked straight at me, never moving his eyes as he too, sat back.

"Our Sun King was crowned King at a very young age. He is a stately man, although of rather small stature. But his strong character makes him a giant among men, and every moment spent in his presence is an honor. His heart shines brightly and he can transform an entire room with his undeniable magnetism.

When the King speaks, he is heard, because everybody stops to listen. When something amuses him, his eyes are bright and dancing. But, if anything bothers him or interferes with his wishes, beware! His clear blue eyes then turn an ice-cold, dark-blue color, usually a presage to a terrible tempest, one that can shake the entire Kingdom. But be assured, this is rare. Most of the time the Sun King is charming and pleasant, especially when entertaining guests, and even more so when he is in the company of his many friends and loving family. Never one to avoid extravagance, our Sun King is lavish and magnanimously hospitable. He always finds time to be generous and benevolent to his invited guests or even with the travelers just passing by. Indeed, well deserved is his fame of an excellent host, the perfect one.

Never one to tire easily, one can find him early in the morning walking around the gardens, lagoons and waterfalls surrounded by his entourage and at midday feasting, with friends and family around the pools. He usually finishes the day off in one of his fabulous dinner banquets that last long into the early hours. How he manages to do it is a mystery to all at first, until you get to know him better. Then its easy to understand. His philosophy is that time is always too short, hence every moment counts. He emphasises constantly that if you could fill each day with work, or service to insure the welfare of others, only then was it a day well used. Never one to waste any minute himself, he definitely practices what he preaches. Another well-known mannerism of this King is his lack of forbearance or strong disapproval towards mediocrity. However, like any wise benevolent King would do, with the same rod he measures others, he uses on himself and his family too, and he lives

THE SUN KING

and acts in accordance to his beliefs. It was well known that not once has he ever judged someone without having before given enough time and opportunity to hear the accused case. But we are aware that his tolerance is not weakness, so we know that if someone fails to follow and respect the Kingdom's law to the best of their personal ability, they risk exile from the beautiful valley and this placid Kingdom, with nothing else but their own person. Maybe this is because the King is so proud of his flourishing Kingdom and wants the people from far and near to respect it also!

When I inquired about his background, Inzer said the Sun King, since a very tender age had been instructed by the greatest mentors of the time. Brought from very far lands specially with the purpose of training him in all the known sciences, including also what he liked best, the difficult trade of bartering. As it usually happens when a young one has the right qualities and enough interest, with the passing of time, he mastered it until he converted it into an art. The royal Sun King was also known by his flawless diplomacy and the excellent relations he effortlessly maintained with all the neighboring nations and tribes. He is a solitary King: there is no queen! Three had existed, but after the third was gone, it seemed the Kingdom would never know another. Inzer very subtly mentioned that only on solemn occasions was it possible to have the Royal family all together. They were very dissimilar in their ages, though that did not matter in the important essence of their family ties. Inzer told me that he had observed many times that whenever they were reunited, it became a happy and festive occassion, and they enjoyed each other immensely. In the center of them all, basking in their love, a proud father: the Sun King.

Another distinguishing characteristic very intrinsic of all the royalty, whether young or old, was although they were direct descendants of Kings, and knew it, they all practiced a rare virtue. One of these virtues was a combination of sincere tolerance and humility which was appreciated not only within their own entourage but the valley residents that lived under their protection. Therefore, it is the perfect combination of wisdom, justice and humility that keeps this land and its ruler in perfect harmony and perpetual happiness, an aura that is felt easily, even to a traveler like you.

I thanked Inzer for his description and asked him to continue and describe the four princesses.

CHAPTER 18

THE FOUR PRINCESSES

Cary is the eldest. She is a bit different from the other three in that she is very scholarly and has always been quick to learn and anxious to acquire even more knowledge. Her short hair is quite lustrous and contrasts with her skin. She has received extra special treatment because of her white birth-mark that resembles a lion's head. A curious coincidence since here in this kingdom, the lion was considered the symbol of liberty. She is humble and regards herself as just another citizen of Chandi. She likes to entertain us with her poetry and readings. We all love her very much.

"The two middle sisters, Lutrania and Kuiosa, are twins. Although they were born on the same day, they are quite different. Lutrania is as white as a lily and her eyes are luminous and mysterious. She maintains an air of royalty about her and, as a result, distances herself from those around her, even her attendants. She is very brooding, as if her thoughts are somewhere else. Kuiosa was born with very dark skin. Her hair is black and falls over her shoulders and cascades down her back.

"Unlike her twin, she is very accessible to all and likes to be sociable. She plays quite a bit with the children of the palace. Also, she is the one person that can bring Lutrania out of her pensive moods, and together they are mischievous enough to keep most of the attendants busy cleaning up after them.

"Finally, there is Retronia, the youngest. Oddly, she is the daughter that has taken upon herself to be responsible for the welfare of the other three. For one so young, she shows great maturity and wisdom far beyond that of her sisters. You will recognize her by her distinctive coloring, neither white, black, or brown, but a golden amber. She, too, has black hair and keeps it cropped very close to her scalp. This gives her face the appearance of being very round, punctuated by deep, brown penetrating eyes. She is quite stunning.

"The runes related prophecies about these daughters, and they all are fulfilled: that one would have a birthmark, that two would be as one, and that the last one would be caretaker of the previous three."

Many more questions played havoc with my mind. I hadn't had much of a chance to write in my journal, and I'm sure many questions I had were lost as one fantastic story followed another. One question gnawed at me; one that Inzer apparently did not have the information to answer. That was, how did I fit into this scenario? What was the reason for my being there, other than being one caught up in the search for The Sun Stone? I hoped that I would stumble across some answers shortly.

Suddenly, at that moment, I became quite concerned about Elizabeth. "Please, tell me what's become of Elizabeth? I need to know that she is safe and that no harm has come to her."

Inzer looked at me and said, "Mr. Bunt, I can promise you that she is safe and will not meet any harm. She has been separated from you for a reason; a reason that even I do not know."

"But surely you know where she has been taken. And who gave the order for her detainment." I said.

"All I know is that someone of great importance made this request. My respect for him allows me to do his bidding without question. Please, let's go. The celebration is about to begin," said Inzer. He walked to the door, opened it, and motioned for me to exit.

CHAPTER 19

THE ROYAL CELEBRATION

"Before we join in the celebration, Inzer said, I think it is important for you to know a few things about the people of our kingdom. Please, come close to my side as we walk".

"In our valley, the Valley of the Sun, there are four groups of residents—all equal in importance and contribution. Each group is organized according to the kind of work they do: there are craftsmen, miners, hunters and merchants. We have no farmers, as food from the earth is plentiful.

"We have, of course, those of noble character who help the Sun King rule effectively and fairly. There are twelve of them and they are known as the Leopards the priests of our kingdom. They advise the Sun King and do so with love and affection. There is one that has powers above all the rest and his name is Mur, a magician. I can not tell you much more about him. He is the keeper of our history and guardian of the sacred scriptures. He has much power and understanding, and he, too, advises the Sun King. You will see him taking part in the celebration."

A gong reverberated almost deafeningly. It must have been the gong whose sound permeated the entire valley yesterday, right before Chawa led us to the Palace.

Inzer led me back to the Elephant Wing of the palace. During our brisk walk, the rumble of drums began, their exact and constant rhythm punctuated the air. We made our way past the large sculptured elephant and out onto the terrace at the top of the Grand Staircase.

"Look. There!" Inzer pointed to an area beyond the Royal Stairs to a structure that appeared to ring an outdoor, sunken amphitheater. "That is the Royal Arena. If you look closely enough, you can see the Gong of the Sun Lion to the right. It will be sounded again at any moment to announce the arrival of the Priests and the Sun King."

No sooner had he said this, that the gong did indeed flourish, and its shimmer crescendoed through the Valley. At that moment, a cheer erupted.

I looked over at Inzer, who was on bended knee, and mumbling something to himself, as was everyone else around me. Suddenly, the gong sounded again. Inzer and the people stood and a great cheer rushed through the crowd.

The Sun King appeared at the highest point of the Royal Stairs. He was dressed in hues of blue and gold in true imitation of the natural colors of a clear blue sky and its ruler: the sun. The Sun King dazzled his audience, even more than the reflection of the many torches that surrounded and illuminated the Royal Stairs. The entire spectacle was so impressive that the people gave an emotional salute of sincere admiration to their ruler. We were all astonished at this magnificence.

Next came the rumble of hundreds of drums, a salute to the barely visible sun in the sky and to their ruler on earth, the Sun King. There was a joyful anticipation among the multitude which spread like wildfire.

Triumphant fanfares gave the cue for the Sun King and his companions to start the procession. Preceding the King came the twelve High Priests of the Kingdom, each accompanied by his own guardian twin—his leopard brother! I was surprised when I discovered Chawa was one of the Priests. Astonished, a hundred questions raced through my mind, but the ceremony continued in spite of my inner turmoil. These very dignified Leopard Priests solemnly descended the stairs. The Leopards' spotted skins were identical to those of their brothers, the animal guardians of the Kingdom. The faces of these extraordinary Priests had feline features. They were scantily dressed, most likely because such astonishing skin like theirs didn't deserve to be hidden. They wore impressive gold pectorals and matching golden bracelets that reflected the sun's light, dazzling the multitude. What caught my attention, in addition to the glorious display of elegance, was the way

Preceding the King came the twelve High Priests of the Kingdom, each accompanied by his own guardian twin—his leopard brother!

in which each of the twelve guardian leopards walked slowly besides their respective Leopard High Priest, occasionally roaring and shaking their heads back and forth. Their descent, though slow and deliberate, was like a silent dance that had been perfectly orchestrated. I later learned, through the manuscripts of the Kingdom's early history, that the Leopard High Priests were highly honored since the very beginning of their time. Their descent down the stairs, I was informed, was always accompanied with chants of praise to the Creator, who surely was impressed with the superb quality of their melodic voices.

I was truly impressed. Never before had I seen such grandiosity or witnessed anything like this. The entire pageant was worthy of the best fantasy. Can you imagine the glorious procession I just described set against a grandiose Palace, a Palace sharply outlined against a soft blue sky that was streaked with a few capricious peach-colored strokes; a Palace surrounded by extraordinary vegetation and the sound of chirping birds, heartfelt chants and melodies? Dozens of lit torches danced happily to the exciting rhythm of the hundred drums. High above, the Sun King awaited.

When the High Priests touched the base of the Royal Stairs, the noble Sun King began his descent. He was gratified that all the people were jubilant, and that they accorded him great respect and admiration. As he walked down, I noticed that his elaborate cape had begun to unfold, until it covered the entire stairway. Inzer pointed out that the cape was embroidered with precious stones and pure gold ornaments. He whispered that the entire history of the Valley of the Sun was told in the embroidery of the cape. I had never seen such splendor and was greatly impressed by this extraordinary cape. I was told sometime later that this was the only occasion in which the Sun King wore it and could be admired by his subjects. I felt truly lucky. Once the Sun King had reached the bottom of the stairs, the whole multitude bowed their heads and pounded their chests with closed fists in tribute to their King. It was easy for me to do the same.

Then the Nobility began their descent. Preceding them, four finely dressed and incredibly beautiful girls began to gather up the King's cape, folding it with care. They surely were aware that this cape carried the story of their people.

Inzer explained that following the Nobles' descent, came the banner procession, which proudly represented the four original tribes. Each one of them displayed their protector and guide. I saw a banner with a portrait of a kudu with enormous sapphire blue eyes, exactly like the one I saw that night at the first camp Chawa and I set up not so long ago! Another banner contained an illustration of a snow white crane with two impressive emerald eyes. Again, identical to the one I thought I had

THE PROCESSION

seen that same night. The third had an outline of a huge elephant with gigantic ivory tusks and the last one portrayed monkeys whose hands overflowed with precious and rare stones. My excitement took Inzer by surprise. He was unaware of my encounters with the kudu and the crane because I hadn't mentioned it to anybody here. But, he knew I was intrigued and tried to satisfy my curiosity by telling me the story behind this last banner and what it represented.

Inzer said the friendly, yet humble monkeys had, since the beginning, always offered to Chandi's inhabitants, the most valuable gift of all: food. Of course, this reminded me of Elizabeth's and my adventure in the Cavern of Rajun, where the monkeys helped Elizabeth and I survive by bringing us fruit.

As the procession drew to a close, twenty dashing young men descended, carrying huge trays of pure gold with intricately engraved ivory handles full of gifts that Sun King would later distribute among his people. Exquisite music enhanced the pageantry and it could be heard, I'm sure, throughout the entire valley. The area surrounding the Palace was trimmed with colorful banners, and what Inzer called the Monkey's Plaza was a riot of flying colors. Adding to this glory rose a marvelous monument known as The Temple of Creation, protected by a majestic sculpture of a giant leopard who silently oversaw the entire scene.

Once the breathtaking ceremony concluded on the Royal Stairs, we gathered around the Fountain of Juveni and enjoyed the warmth of the sunny day. A bit to the extreme right, I found the plaza and a grand open-air theater where the Sun King, the Priests, and the populous sat and enjoyed a dialogue outlining and discussing projects for the coming year.

Inzer told me that the Kingdom's wealth came from a very productive Gold, Silver and iron-mining industry. I also noticed that the primary method of exchange was through bartering, and much gold and iron was traded, as well as ivory, wood and ostrich feathers.

Inzer proudly proclaimed that this monarchic dynasty was over two thousand years old. Their longevity, he said, was because the village people and the Nobility had lived together in peace and harmony; each happy with the special place set aside for him where he could ply his own trade, a trade each freely chose, and where everyone was respectful of their neighbors' rights.

All morning I witnessed the frank discussion of how to plan and solve the small and big troubles of the village. Once everything was settled to the entire satisfaction of all, I followed the entire multitude up to the palace. There, I was invited to join the King, Nobles, High Priests, and the rest of the townsfolk to share the most exotic viands and opulent dishes, prepared by the village women.

All of the guests were asked to wait at the sable fountain, a beautiful fountain that displays the heads of six bronzed sable bucks with their large curved horns. The over-sized heads sat on a cylindrical stone base. These heads spill water through the curved arches of the bucks' horns, which were embellished with a harmonious series of arches in a beautiful courtyard.

From where I was standing, I could see up to the main dome, which featured a copper-green finish and rope and frond motifs that created a crown style dome. These were flanked by kudu and crane towers that majestically stood before us, exuding a sense of power that I had heretofore never experienced.

It was a beautiful display of architecture; a delightful view of nature that displayed elaborate carved sculptures of animals and fronds motifs.

I would have to call the architecture of this Palace a classical jungle baroque. I was very impressed with the exterior of this magnificent palace and couldn't wait to see the interior decoration.

Suddenly, at the sound of a gong and to the rhythm of a hundred drums, two bronze doors were opened by four guards. Very slowly, the doors gave way to a ray of light that exploded from the interior.

The golden glow of the sun began to appear as we walked into the main rotunda dome. It was a beautiful space where six columns supported the main interior dome, on whose ceiling was painted a fresco that displayed a jungle scene featuring several types of animals: lions, zebras, elephants, hyenas, and monkeys.

Eighteen rectangular windows beneath the dome gave way to the sun's rays, splashing on the polished marble, slick and shiny. Each piece was cut into the shape of an animal and carefully pieced together. I bent down and trailed my hand gently across the area of floor in front of me, replete with more animal motifs. It was a magnificent space that served as only a hint of what awaited me.

The main space was breath taking. A beautiful, baroque interior dazzled before me. The main area, which was called the Crystal Court, was thirty meters long, about thirty-five meters wide and twelve meters high. It was just one of many beautiful spaces in this Palace. On three sides of this magnificent hall, in groups of five, was a rhythmic colonnade of palm arches and reeds columns. A beautiful, scenic view of a lake and the surrounding jungle and water cascades was the highlight of the Crystal Court.

The view from where I was standing gave me the opportunity to see far to the horizon of the Valley of the sun. It was exhilarating. This space had a beautiful bal-

THE SABLE FOUNTAIN

ance of interior and exterior architecture.

At the top of the grand stairs, to the right and left of me, were two carved, jade columns, visually framing a large, bowl-shaped fountain. Located in the center of the lower, level, this fountain received water from the trunks of four, sculpted, life-sized bronze elephants. Similar bowls were displayed at each corner of this space, each boasting a beautiful arrangement of flowers.

Above, an incredible chandelier of crystal palms, with four semi-curved domes in gold leaf, dominated the room.

We were seated at the table of honor. Suddenly, a second sound of a gong announced the entrance of the Sun King.

The Sun King descended down main stairs and was seated at the center of the room. The sun was at the horizon and the sound of many drums, flutes and strings announced the beginning of the festivities.

Then we were implored to look towards the island across the lagoon. I saw men with torches make their way towards the front of the lake. There, barges waited for a procession of young maids and hunters. This was the ceremony in which all the young ladies of the realm were invited to entertain the palace guests with their fantastic dances. They performed what they called "The Dance of the Sunset." It was a beautiful display of excellent rhythmical movements.

The gong sounded for a third time, heralding the entrance of twenty-six maids. They entered the room from above the two sides of the main stairs, and were dressed exquisitely. They brought with them trays and trays of exotic food. Then came another twenty-six maids who served the food. As they served wine, the King stood up and honored his guests by saying "Welcome to Chandi".

My encounters with the royal family was intriguing. My imagination was fueled to such a degree that I anticipated the pleasure of getting to know them better. Dressed in a kaleidoscope of bright colors, they all appeared to respect each other. Together, they made a perfectly charming family. The daughters were kind, sincere, peace loving people, and fully aware of their position of privilege. They worried about little except for the well-being of their loving father, the Sun King. Very early in their lives they had been taught respect to their elders, and it was interesting to see even the youngest curtsy before their father. I found them intelligent and fun-loving. It would seem impossible to find their presence boring or superfluous. The entire royal family were friendly and at ease in conversation, and the hours passed quickly. We dined and celebrated until the early morning.

CHAPTER 20

THE LEOPARD'S BIRTH

I awoke the next morning to find Inzer at my door, flushed with urgency.

"Hurry," he said, "Please, you must help us. Come quickly!"

I hastily dressed while quizzing him about what was going on.

Inzer explained that an expectant female leopard had just taken up residence at the front entrance to his and Tani's house. As I had seen many leopards walking around loose, I inquired as to why this was different.

"It's Tani," wheezed Inzer, increasing his pace. "She's the one."

"I don't understand," I said. "She's. . . .what?

According to Inzer, everyone was now sure she was the one chosen to give birth to a new leopard-twin baby.

"It is written," explained Inzer, as we neared his abode, "in the Kingdom's oldest manuscripts that two leopard-twin babies—future High Priests of our Kingdom—are born every fifty-two years. Each baby has unusual characteristics. First, the skin is spotted, very much like the coat of the leopard. The face, though not spotted, bears an extraordinary resemblance to a cat. These babies share the leopard's keen eyesight and sense of smell. These leopard babies are of great importance because, when fully grown, they help protect this Kingdom. They are respected and feared by everyone."

Inzer quickened his pace, but continued to rasp his story.

"Both this mother leopard and Tani will give birth at the same time. Our baby is to become a High Priest and will be spiritually joined to the baby leopard, which will be his loyal guardian until the end of their time.

As we approached their stone house, I could see a group of villagers gathered around the heavily-breathing leopard. Inzer was informed that she was about to give birth.

I stopped dead in my tracks. "Wait a minute," I said. "I certainly won't get near a she-leopard when she is giving birth. Forget it. That's way too dangerous."

"Forget the mother leopard," Inzer snapped. "Follow me." He pushed open the ornate wooden door, and beckoned to me.

He was met immediately by a Leopard High Priest.

"We have two problems, Inzer," informed the priest. "First, Tani is having problems with her labor. There's something wrong. Second, our messenger found Be-Lar ill with a high fever. He is unable to help himself, much less poor Tani."

"Be-Lar? Who's Be-Lar? I interjected.

Inzer turned to me. "Be-Lar is our medicine man."

"There's something else," said the High Priest. "In Be-Lar's feverish delirium, he kept repeating our guest's name over and over. That he was the one to help Tani."

"This can't be," I protested, insisting that I was unable to help and certainly unqualified. Although I had observed difficult labors in my travels, I was always appreciative of the natural instincts of the midwives or the medicine men. Either they had a lot of practice, or were born with special gift. The fact was, they invariably saved lives with a lot of faith, a few incantations, and the application of exotic herb mixtures. But at the moment, this was of little comfort to me.

My protestations were to no avail. Since the village medicine man had designated me, there was no way out. Again, the question tormented me: Why and how did we come to be here? It's almost like we were expected. But why?

At that moment I thought of one of my life's philosophies: If you can escape, start running! But if you can't, confront the situation and deal with it. You'll finish sooner.

Inzar's pleading look touched my heart. I thought to myself, someone wanted this to happen and, by God, I would try my best to do it. I followed the Priests to where Tani lay. Once there, I breathed deeply and I asked the women to boil water and to bring clean cloths, a sharp knife and some strong thread. I was sweating profusely and wiped my brow with my sleeves before rolling them up to my elbows. I pretended I was in absolute control of the situation. Nobody moved.

A heavy silence grew heavier by the minute. The light from outside barely illuminated the room. I asked that candles be lit. The flickering light washed over Tani's suffering face. I had to do something... fast. I demanded everyone leave the room. Everyone left except for the two High Priests and Tani's mother. They retreated to the front of the small room and waited near the door. I forgot about them when Tani let out two painful moans, exhausted from the efforts of labor.

Tani's mother murmured, "The baby is either upside down or tangled with the cord. He just won't be born easily."

Something inside of me stirred. My instinct for survival?

Tani cried out loudly. I drew near her. Her forehead was beaded with perspiration. Her big belly was hard as a rock. I felt overwhelmed and completely inadequate.

Tani started to panic as an intense contraction pushed the breath out of her. When it subsided she whimpered that if the baby was dead, she wanted to die, too.

I knew I had to calm Tani, so I whispered to her softly and wiped her forehead with cool cloths rinsed in fresh water. I felt her swollen belly carefully and knew that the baby was headed down the birth canal. Then, with a sudden rush, the water bag broke, flooding the linen and pillows around her. I took a deep breath. Whatever was going to happen, I would have to make a move now!

I pushed on Tani's belly with my left hand and tried to grasp the baby's head with my right. I attempted to turn him to the right, praying that he could be delivered normally. Anxiously, I felt for the umbilical cord, only to find that the cord was around his neck. With time working against me, I considered the alternatives. Too late! The baby began to crown.

"Please, God, please help us!" I prayed under my breath.

With one hand, I tried to hold the slippery tiny head. It struggled to push through but was held back by the cord. Then, using two fingers from my other hand, I gently tried to unwrap the cord from around the baby's neck. The fluid was so slippery that it was hard to hold onto anything. The cord slipped from my fingers and Tani moaned again. I reached in and tried again. This time, I was able to get a tight hold on the cord and managed to loosen it to some degree. Anticipating the moment, Tani's mother handed me the knife. Gently, but quickly, I inserted the knife and severed the cord. One more mighty contraction, and the small being entered the world.

It was an unforgettable moment. The crying, wiggling baby emerged into my waiting hands. Time seemed to stand still. Without losing a second, I tied off the umbilical cord with a piece of thread. The new grandmother immediately covered him with a warm piece of clean cloth. In seconds, she was at my side with a washbasin of lukewarm water for the baby's first bath. She finished, placed the small child on Tani's stomach and left, followed by the two High Priests.

Tani was crying both from pain and the joy of delivery. She grabbed my hand and squeezed it, and I smiled. The baby's first cry was like celestial music to my ears. The robust infant was now crying his heart out. He seemed fine: moving closed fists and kicking hard, turning his tiny head both ways, opening his arms and mouth in search of his mother's breast. More importantly, at least to the High Priests, he showed the signs of being the newest member of the Leopard High

Priests dynasty. His skin showed it, as did his facial features. This was no ordinary baby!

The High Priests were certain prophecy had fulfilled itself once again. The Kingdom's security had been assured a bit longer. Although numbed by the strange sequence of events, I did recognize the importance of the moment. What troubled me was my forced participation and the reasons for it.

I emerged from the hut to find Inzer and the entire village waiting outside. Standing next to Inzer, with an inimical expression, was the beautiful Charir. Everyone else was smiling and some patted my back in congratulations.

In the middle of this joyous moment, I looked over to see the proud mother leopard calmly licking and cleaning her tiny, newborn cub, who suckled hungrily at her teat. Could this small, newborn cub realize his importance to this Kingdom?

At that moment, a powerful roar emerged from the mother's throat and she fixed her eyes on mine. The mother leopard knew, and that was enough.

I removed my hat and bowed low in respect to the other new mother, and answered her steady stare with a wink.

"Congratulations!" I said. I turned to look into the valley's horizon, surprised to find it was now late afternoon.

CHAPTER 21

THE OBSERVATORY

I decided to take a different route back to the palace to enjoy the view from the magnificent Observatory.

It was built in a cleverly calculated niche, between the Great Fountain of Juveni and the impressive Trevor Waterfall. It was strategically situated so that it faced the official "Entrance" to Chandi, the name given to the twin hills that framed the gateway into this splendid valley. From near or far, anyone could easily find the valley by looking for the twin hills. I was almost at the top of the stairs that lead to the Observatory when I heard a familiar voice.

"Mr. Bunt, hey, Mr. Bunt. Here!" I turned to my right to find a smiling man they called Wanner.

Wanner, who I had met at the first feast, was a fan of the god's exquisite nectars and distilled spirits, which, when combined, would make a beverage that would often intoxicate quickly. Wanner tried hard to hide his love of drink, but he was pleasant, and extremely easy to talk to.

Surprisingly, tonight he looked tense, but feigned nonchalance as he carefully surveyed our surroundings. I got the impression he didn't want anybody to see us here together. Nonetheless, I followed him.

He led the way into the Observatory. Wanner said that this magical site was created by Prince Shukan as a celestial surveillance zone, after returning with his tribe from the great Northlands. It was here that the High Priests traced their maps of the visible stars in the sky and studied astronomy. A circular structure, the walls and domed ceiling were dotted with impressive engravings which appeared to depict what seemed to be constellations, all strangely related to animal forms.

As I tried to figure out what it all meant, Wanner's muted voice interrupted my thoughts.

"Come here. Please keep quiet and pay attention," he demanded.

His nervousness was very apparent, so I only nodded and obediently kept quiet. He uncovered an instrument and beckoned me to it.

Curious, I looked through the instrument, which was a simple, primitive telescope. In this early darkness I thought I saw the moon and said so, only to be corrected.

"No," said Wanner, "you're wrong. That is Venurton, a very important star. She is wife to our beloved Sun, our Sustainer and Life Protector. She follows our mother earth wherever she goes. You see, she is responsible for our tides, birthing cycles and, most important, she lights our way through the darkest nights."

It was amusing to hear Wanner explain this. With the help of his rudimentary instrument, he described, in a few simple and poetic words, many things that scientists were discovering and taking credit for back home. I was very interested and keen to continue our talk about his discoveries when, from outside, strange sounds distracted us.

Mur, the Kingdom's Magician, approached. He was encircled by seven big torches carried by the same torch bearers who accompanied the Sun King to his nightly banquets. But tonight, they showed the way for Mur.

"What is going on?" Mur demanded.

Wanner hid the instrument behind his back. He was trembling from head to toe. I waited.

Mur extended his right hand, with no word of greeting or admonishment. Wanner obediently placed the rudimentary telescope in Mur's hand. Without a word or acknowledgment of my presence, the Magician turned and left.

I looked at Wanner, who looked as if the blood had drained from his face. He sat down on the solid rock floor. For a moment, I didn't know what to do. Should I help Wanner? Or should I follow the Magician and find out for myself what had just happened and why? Mur disappeared down the carved stairway next to the fountain of Juveni.

"Wanner? What happened just now? Are you feeling all right?" I inquired.

He opened his eyes wide and wiggled his eyebrows. "Is he gone?"

"Yes," I answered. "He's gone."

He removed a cloth from his pocket and dabbed at his now-sweaty forehead. "Oh, well, that wasn't too bad."

I sat down next to him and quickly evaluated his mental health. Most likely, I thought to myself, Wanner would never be more than a charming, albeit naughty, happy-go-lucky star-gazer.

Enveloped in complete darkness now, we sat on the floor, feeling a little like two small children who had just been caught stealing a cookie. The absurdity of it all caused us both to laugh out loud.

After a while, silence fell upon us once again. The night sky seemed to carry more stars than usual. During my travels in the Dark Continent, I, too, had become an avid star-gazer. Yet tonight, there were definitely more stars in the ebony night sky. From The Observatory, it was easy to see across the whole valley, over which I slowly ran my eyes. It was then that I saw Inzer on the next hill. He was carrying a torch and heading towards the Temple of Courage. I immediately got to my feet and pointed this out to Wanner.

"Let's follow him," I implored of Wanner, but he flatly refused, saying it would be dangerous for me to do so. Wanner begged me to stay with him, to share some of his favorite beverage. I thanked him for his kind invitation but turned and left. I bounded out of The Observatory and walked in the darkness, towards the lagoon. I wondered if I could cross the Spider's Hanging Bridge on such a dark night. I was determined to find out as much as I could about the mysterious goings-on of this strange and beautiful kingdom. I can only help us, I thought, by learning as much as I can.

CHAPTER 22

THE TEMPLE OF COURAGE

Though I kept my distance, I managed to follow Inzer all the way to the Baobab Forest and see him join a procession. I paused to catch my breath and to determine my proximity to them. They weren't too far away. I saw a circle of torches and was surprised to see that they surrounded Mur. He was accompanied by two Leopard High Priests.

I waited a bit longer to be sure I hadn't been detected, then continued to follow them. A short time later, I came upon a rock formation that provided both a good lookout and promising refuge. I was confident that I was hidden well enough until I felt breath on my neck. My heart raced as I quickly jumped to my left. I turned to discover I had company. To my relief, it was Samo—the small monkey, my faithful old friend. He obviously was equally as happy to see me and began jumping up and down, making loud, screeching noises.

"Sh! Ssh!" I implored. I grabbed him and covered his mouth. He instantly calmed.

I looked around for something to distract him and keep him occupied. I searched my pockets and found two nuts I had earlier snatched from the fruit tray in my quarters. I gave them to him and patted his tiny head to make sure he stayed next to me in silence. Thankfully, it worked.

Once again, I turned my attention to Mur and the procession, wondering what was taking place. It was then that I remembered that Inzer had mentioned a ceremony in which the Kingdom's hunters were initiated into that special group.

Apparently, it was celebrated only once a year on a very special night. All the young men of the Kingdom were eager candidates, as hunters held a position of honor and privilege in the kingdom. Unfortunately, only a few endured the trials of the initiation ceremony conducted at the Temple of Courage. Those who did were declared members of the Kingdom's Hunters.

In the company of my tiny friend, I continued my surveillance.

Once the procession had reached the top of the hill, hundreds of new torch lights burst into flames and completely surrounded the fabulous Temple, illuminating it in an eerie and magical atmosphere. The long stairway was also illuminated, and from my vantage point, seemed as though a wild river of fire cascaded down it. All of this grand spectacle reflected on the lagoon below, which lay calm and shiny like a mirror.

The Leopard High Priests, in leopard-skin loincloths and ornamented in their gold and silver splendor, stood on a ramp to the right side, high above a group of nearly forty Hunter candidates.

One by one, each aspirant was led to a wall into which the face of an open-mouthed lion was carved. Smoke poured from its nostrils, and the chants and deafening rumble of drums turned my skin to goose flesh. As each young man's turn arrived, he approached the carving and plunged his tightly-closed right fist inside the giant, sculpted mouth. Each time, the drumming intensified, and each time its savageness awakened something primitive deep inside of me. This feeling began to envelope me until I felt as if I had become part of the ceremony, too. I watched intently.

Mur and one of the Leopard High Priests stood on either side of a hopeful candidate and whispered something into his ear. The earth tremored slightly and a horrible grinding sound emanated from the depths of the mountain every time a candidate was tested. The inside of the sculpted lion's mouth was brightly illuminated, as if a terrible fire was burning inside. Smoke and vapor surged through the opening, completely enveloping Mur, the Priest and each candidate. The heat must have been unbearable.

It appeared that if the candidate willingly placed his right fist inside the lion's mouth, he was taken inside the Temple. Each time this was the case, cries of victory from the rest of the aspiring candidates and the High Priests pierced the air. Unfortunately, I couldn't get a glimpse of what happened inside. The great majority of the young men quickly pulled their bloody fists from the lion's mouth, grimacing and crying out painfully. Those who didn't were dutifully led down the stairway and back toward the village. I remember Chawa saying that every young man who stood for initiation was held in great respect, even if he failed. He would be allowed to find another craft or trade in which he could use his talents to benefit the Kingdom. Failure only meant that the candidate wasn't ordained to be a hunter.

Before long, the group of forty soon dwindled, and only thirteen had entered into the Temple. One by one, from inside the Temple, each had been called by name to the entrance. From my vantage point, I witnessed the presentation of the thirteen initiates. Again, furious drum music began and an unbearable sound of falling rock filled the air. All around me, the earth shook and the tall trees swayed. I covered my head, hoping to avoid being clunked on the head. As the Temple's walls shook and rattled, the floor of the Temple opened to reveal a small, circular platform surrounded by several enormous tongues of fire. One by one, each of the thirteen initiates crossed through the fire. Strangely, they were neither burned nor showed any outward signs of pain. As the final initiate took his place on the stone platform, an eerie silence followed. No one moved. The twelve Leopard High Priests walked around the burning platform several times, invoking the same incantation over and over. Though I could see only the twelve Priests mouth the words, it seemed as if the number of voices increased. Although I saw only the candidates, Mur and the High Priests, it sounded as if hundreds of voices had joined in. Then, abruptly, they stopped. At that moment, I saw a Leopard High Priest approach the pillars of fire and, magically, pull hunting weapons from the flames: knives, darts, and golden shields. Red from the heat of the fire, neither the Leopard High Priests nor the initiates balked at handling the steaming metal. Each initiate received three weapons and a body shield and, once fully dressed in their body shield and armed with their new weapons, they saluted the High Priests and Mur. Then a strange thing occurred. Mur led the hunters to the edge of the temple's platform and, one by one, they jumped off and plunged down the Temple's cascading waterfall—a freefall of probably thirty nine meters.

I recalled Inzer's words: the hunter who was the first to arrive at the Palace the following morning to embark on their first hunting trip would be named leader of the new group.

The last initiate had plunged down through the falls. Mur and his High Priests spoke among themselves, the light in the temple dimmed. The ritual was over. I didn't know if my witnessing this ceremony had equipped me with any new knowledge I could use, but later, I wrote in my journal that I thought the essential element of these young men's quest was bravery beyond reason. Sometime later, with Mur's help, I found out that hero-hunters were subjected to many different tests to prove them worthy and they were instructed how to live without compromise in the quest of good. Only after successfully enduring these rigors were they allowed to be hunters for the rest of their lives.

CHAPTER 23

THE ROYAL FEAST

I rested and wrote in my journal the better part of the next day. I was to be a guest at a royal feast in the Crystal Palace. Strangely, after seeming to be someone expected, someone special, and even someone needed—thinking of the "twin" leopard birthing—I was left completely alone all day. I tried piecing together all the mysteries of this place, and wondered if something important would be revealed at the royal feast.

As the night exchanged places with another day, the gong sounded, summoning all to the feast.

Just as I reached the Crystal Court, in the distance the gong sounded for the third and final time, swelling in volume. Immediately, the drumming began again, originating somewhere beyond the reflecting pool in front of the Crystal Court. The pulsating beat caused the celebrating Chandians to sway back and forth in rhythm.

The bright colors of their gowns against the splendor of the Crystal Court was like a living collage that shifted randomly before my eyes. Inzer saw me enter and rose to invite me to a seat beside his own. I was about to ask him about Tani, when I was interrupted as huge platters of exotic fruits, nuts and meats were passed among us, and drink flowed freely.

Again I turned to Inzar, but at this time, the Sun King stood and held his hand up. Immediately, the drumming stopped and the music faded into silence.

All eyes were on the Sun King. Inzer reached over and tapped me on the shoulder. "Listen." he said. "Our King is going to make an offering to God and extol the sacred Sun Stone. He's also going to introduce Lanier, his fiancée, to the Kingdom.

The Sun King spoke:

"Citizens of Chandi and honorable guests, I greet you and wish upon thee all kinds of blessings from our Sustainer, who has so graciously sanctioned us not only with this, our beautiful land, but with our precious Sun Stone which attests to our heritage and our history. Through this treasure we know who we are and from where we have come. For this we are thankful. Hence, we find it right to offer today on this happy celebration our sincere gratitude and never-ending adoration to the All-Merciful."

The Sun King turned to Mur, the high priest, who stepped forward and offered to the King a crystal orb from whose center shot rays of gold and red that reflected off of the ceiling and walls of the Crystal Court. The Sun King took the orb and held it high over his head as he mumbled a few words.

Strangely, as he spoke to himself, the crowd before him parted, leaving a clear view of the reflecting pool beyond the pillars. He lowered the orb and cradled it for a moment. Then, in one motion, he hurled the sphere toward the reflecting pool where it splashed loudly as it broke the surface. After a few moments, the pool began to bubble fiercely and the crowd cheered. Then, just as quickly, the pool again became serene and calm. All eyes again fixed on the Sun King.

He again looked to the sky and said in a firm voice, "Almighty, you have promised us prosperity and peace, and we have rejoiced in it. When you have turned your blessing away from us we fully accepted it as our own fault. Yet not even then have you abandoned us without also giving us the hope of recovering your grace, once our lesson is learned. Today, a noble woman, with the intelligence of a scholar, the heart of a lion and the beauty of a virgin, has taken my heart away. The runes speak about a woman, a stranger to our land, with the eyes the color of the bluest sky, who shall come to marry a Sun King. So now the time has come, I beg with a humble heart Thou blessing in my decision to marry the fairest of them all: Lanier, the ruler of my heart."

I looked all over the place for this woman, of whom, before now, I had never heard. She was easy to identify. Indeed her beauty was worthy of legends... Lanier had no sooner acknowledged Sun King's reference to her with a suitable smile, when she looked directly at me with cold disdainful eyes. Surprised, I looked away, feeling very uncomfortable. Oblivious of everything else but his new found happiness, Sun King turned to his four daughters with open arms. Each, one after the other, came forward to hug the King and kiss him on the cheek. A sign of acceptance, I gathered.

Only then did Sun King turned to Lanier to offer his embrace. But alas! Instead of rising and approaching the Sun King in a show of subservience, as we expected, she held out her hand, beckoning the King to approach her instead! Amazingly, he did just that.

I looked around me. I happened to see Mur looking quite distraught. He looked at the ground and shook his head, ever so slightly. No one noticed. All the others, including Chawa, did not seem to be put off by this display. For me, it was a troubling moment; both awkward and strange. I turned to find Inzer looking fiercely at me. I started to speak, but he quickly held up his finger to his lips to discourage any utterance.

As the Sun King rose to his feet, another loud cheer erupted from the multitudes and immediately the music began again. The tense moment quickly evaporated into merry-making and dancing. Lost in the spirit of the party, I relaxed and quickly joined in the celebration.

Before us an area had been cleared away. Right in front of the Elephant Fountain, a number of young, female dancers appeared. The tempo of the music changed and became more lively. To the delight of the Sun King and the others, these dancers began to sway and contort to the music, synchronized and well-rehearsed. I was captivated by the skill with which these girls leaped and bounded around the floor.

Someone handed me a large plate filled with cheeses and meats. I took what I could and set it in my lap, preparing to eat. Suddenly, at that moment, one of the young dancers leapt up the two stairs to where I was sitting, took my hand and easily pulled me to my feet, causing the food to spill onto several of the pillows I had been propped up against.

She dragged me to the middle of the floor and the other dancers circled and began to dance around me. I looked at the crowd, and could only see smiles and a myriad of colors playing against each other. The drumming and music got louder and the people began to clap in rhythm, urging the girls on. They continued to circle me as I spun around, trying to gather my senses. The girls that had pulled me to the dance floor reached toward me, offering me their hands. Suddenly, a young dancer offered me her hand and I took it. Off we went, spinning around and around to the beat of the drums, which steadily increased in volume and intensity.

I threw caution to the wind, and began to laugh. The dancer held my hands tightly and she pulled back as we spun, causing us to go faster and faster. Suddenly, I became quite dizzy. The beautiful dancer let me go and I staggered about, much to the delight of those watching. I couldn't maintain my balance and fell in a heap to the floor.

When I hit the ground, I heard a distinctive sound, as if glass had hit the floor. Immediately, deadly silence enveloped the gathering, the kind of quiet before a storm. Still groggy, I made it up to my knees, the room continuing to swirl around me, silently. When I focused, I looked about to find every eye in the Crystal Court fixed on me. Or to be more exact, fixed on what lay on the floor before me.

The crystal was about a meter in front of me. It had become dislodged during my dancing and spinning and had fallen out of my shirt. I quickly grabbed it and put it back inside my pocket. I slowly raised my head, praying that the deafening silence was a figment of my imagination. No such luck.

Inzer was quickly at my side and offered me his hand, which I took and hoisted myself to my feet. Still somewhat disoriented, Inzer led me back to the group of pillows and helped me lower myself into their false comfort.

Gradually, the drumming and music began again, and it wasn't too long before it seemed this little incident was forgotten to everyone else. Or so I had hoped. Nonetheless, I was somewhat concerned about the hush that had fallen over the throng. Was it because of my inept crash to the floor? Or was it that the crystal was exposed? As I had no idea, I was forced to conduct myself as if nothing had happened.

I looked at those around me. Most everyone had returned to their celebrating. The Sun King approached me to see if I was unharmed. He said nothing about the crystal and seemed merely concerned that I had not injured myself. I smiled and reassured him that I was fine, and apologized for my clumsiness.

My eyes darted to those around him. Most were talking, laughing, and intent on making the most of the celebration. That's when my eyes met Mur, the chief priest. He looked at me and, for some reason, I saw a hint of anticipation deep in his eyes. His gaze lasted only a moment before he looked away, and then quickly whispered something to his attendant. He then turned and left. I turned and looked over my shoulder. Lanier's cold eyes locked on mine again! Quickly, I looked away to the celebrating masses before me. I tried to act nonchalant so that no one would suspect my misgivings and mindlessly picked at my food.

The celebration had again reached an intensity that is reserved for only the most special of occasions. The people were happy and unmindful of anything but the festivities.

Inzer leaned over to me and said, "You can see how much the people like to celebrate. It is something that we all enjoy. My parents and their parents before them all took part in celebrations very similar to this one."

I nodded in agreement although my mind was elsewhere, sorting out my eerie misgivings. Fear gnawed at me. It was then that I wondered about Elizabeth's safety, since she was nowhere to be seen at this celebration.

A short, stumpy fellow with very black skin and oddish light brown eyes made his way through the group of people behind us, and pushed gently but forcefully to Inzer's side. He took a seat next to Inzer and cupped his hand over Inzer's ear. Whatever he had whispered to Inzer was brief, for he stood and quickly pushed his way back through the wall of people. Turning to Inzer, I saw my own misgivings reflected in his eyes.

CHAPTER 24

MUR THE MAGICIAN

"Please, follow me, Mr. Bunt. There is someone who would very much like to speak with you," Inzer directed rather formally.

"Can't we do it later? I'm trying to see if Elizabeth is here," I objected. My eyes scanned the crowd hopefully.

"I'm sorry, Mr. Bunt, but this person is very, very important. To keep him waiting would be very disrespectful, not to mention unwise," Inzer admonished.

I grabbed Inzer's extended hand and pulled myself up from the pillows. I touched my shirt and felt the crystal warmly lodged in its folds. I followed Inzer as the pressing crowd opened a pathway for him. We turned down the spacious hallway toward the Elephant Wing of the Palace.

"Where are we going, Inzer? Is everything all right? I inquired. "Why the urgency?"

"I don't know why, but you have been summoned by Mur, the Chief Priest and Magician to the Sun King.

"To have a private audience with him should be considered a high honor, and one that you would do well to heed," he advised. His new attitude was quite evident.

I followed Inzer closely. He had quickened his gait. We passed through the Elephant Wing, by the very life-like sculpted elephant, and across the outside terrace that was moist with the spray from the fountain. We found ourselves at the top of the Royal Staircase. Inzer began to descend the stairs.

"Wait!" I said excitedly. "I thought we're not supposed to use these stairs. What of the leopards that guard them? Don't they cause you any concern?"

"Stay near to me and no harm will come to you," he said, pulling me close to his side.

We made it to the bottom of the staircase without incident; not even a growl from any of the leopards. Without any hesitation, Inzer followed the path, bearing right. We passed the Royal Arena, which was more of a sunken hole. The pillars surrounding it were topped by horizontal slabs that connected each pillar to the next. I stopped and looked up to the far side of the arena to see the immense golden gong swaying slowly from two supports made of the biggest elephant tusks I had ever seen.

Inzer tugged at me. "Hurry. We mustn't keep Mur waiting."

He led me down a few stairs and continued about a hundred meters until we reached another steep stairway. Inzer rapidly ascended and I followed.

At the top of the stairs was a large terraced area that had a fountain. From the middle of a pool, on a rock base, were four sculpted monkeys, each facing to a point on the compass. They had outstretched hands, and the water spilled out of their palms into the pool below. I looked behind me to see the Palace in the distance, rising from the jungle floor, its minarets reaching boldly towards the stars.

"Where are we, Inzer?" I asked curiously.

"This is the Monkey Springs Plaza. It was constructed in honor of monkeys who gathered fruit for our ancestors. If it weren't for the monkeys, we might not be standing here today," he explained, "as a fierce drought in ancient times almost starved our people into extinction. But, come, we mustn't delay. It isn't much farther. We must cross the Bridge of Time to where Mur awaits us in the Temple of Creation."

We headed across the Bridge of Time, which was guarded by stone elephants sculptures fashioned from gray rock, five to each side of the walkway. Their tusks were of polished ivory. Each elephant stood proudly on the top of a large square platform. At the far end of the bridge was the head of an elephant, carved into the granite, right above a dark hole that disappeared into the belly of the mountain. I was queasy as I looked over the side of the Bridge of Time. I heard a deep rumbling, like thunder, rising from the depths of the deep gorge that the Bridge of Time spanned. There was so much steam and vapor that I could not see the bottom of this crevasse.

I followed Inzer into the black hole that poked into the rock façade. Our path was illuminated only by the light of a few dimly burning torches protruding from the walls of the tunnel. We ascended a few spiral staircases to the Temple of Creation.

At its center was a large round slab of marble supported by a single cylinder of gold. At one side of the slab stood a man with the skin of ebony and a leopard's green eyes. He was about my height but was stooped at the waist, as if the burden of the world were on his shoulders. His hair was white and flowed from the side of his head onto his shoulders. The top of his head was bald although I never notice this before, because he always wore an ornate hat in public. He also carried a pectoral similar to the one Chawa and all the other priests wore. His, however, had a

MUR THE MAGICIAN AND ALAN BUNT

large diamond glowing in its center.

Inzer bowed and supplicated himself on one knee. "Great Magician Mur, may I introduce to you Mr. Alan Bunt."

Unsure about what was expected of me `I stretched out my hand in greeting. As he stood, Mur reached for my hand and pulled me towards the marble table. In its middle was a chest made of gold, embedded with many gems of red, blue, green and yellow.

"Please, Mr. Bunt, be seated. It is good that you came to see me," Mur said with a deep, modulated tone. "I'm sure you are curious as to why I called for you."

"I'm curious about many things. Ever since I met Chawa at a watering hole outside the township of Baratu much has been unexplainable. Mr. Mur.....

"Please. My name is Mur, not Mr. Mur." He nodded to Inzer, who bowed and started towards the stairs to take his leave.

"Inzer! I ....." Inzer interrupted me.

"I'm sorry, Mr. Bunt, but I must go. I might be missed and I am leaving you in very able hands."

He pulled the golden chest towards him and opened it.

Before I could protest further, Inzer bounded down the stairs. That would be the last time I ever saw him. I sat in the chair, across from Mur, uncertain of my fate.

Mur began. "Mr. Bunt, I can assure you that, for now, you have nothing to worry about. However, it is very important that you listen to what I must say. Then, if you still feel threatened and uneasy, we will address that which disturbs you."

"And Elizabeth?"

"Ah, yes, your lovely traveling companion. I know you must be worried about her but I will tell you that I saw her just this morning and she is well cared for."

"What? You saw Elizabeth? She's not hurt, is she?" I asked.

"As I said, she is fine. I believe that you will know the reason for her being separated from you after I have told you what must be said," he stated pointedly.

"Very well," I answered.

"Mr. Bunt, first I must inform you that I have been hoping for your appearance for a very long time. You are special to the Kingdom of Chandi. Even if you don't understand me, let me tell you just one more thing, our continued existence may depend on your reaction to what I am about to tell you."

I was still skeptical. Eyeing Mur closely, I leaned to the middle of the table.

"I'm most anxious to hear, Mur. Tell me what I don't know. Tell me why I'm so important to Chandi. Tell me why I have no idea where it is or have ever heard of it before." I looked him directly in the eye, but Mur didn't flinch.

He pulled the golden chest towards him and opened it.

CHAPTER 25

THE THREE SCROLLS

As Mur removed the lid of the chest, a great light filled the room. Mur's face was illuminated by the golden glow which softened the chiseled features of his face. His eyes grew wide as he reached into the chest and removed three scrolls. I looked into the chest to see many other scrolls, perhaps twenty-six, each a different color, each rolled up tightly and secured with a golden braid—a braid exactly like the one Chawa had given me. The scrolls Mur removed was made of parchment: one yellow, one blue, and one green. Mur placed the scrolls out on the table, still bound.

Mur went on as he fingered one of the scrolls. "Before I answer any of your questions, it would be best for you to look at these," he said, motioning to the scrolls. "These hold the answer to many of your questions, although I'm certain they will raise new ones as well."

Mur's face was illuminated by the golden glow which softened the chiseled features of his face.

"This yellow parchment has never been opened and read because only you are permitted to do so," he said.

"Me?" I asked. "Why me? I'm nothing more than a man with a passion for adventure. How can it be that I am to open this scroll?"

"The crystal, Mr. Bunt. The crystal."

"The crystal?" I reacted by feeling for it under my shirt.

"When I saw that crystal that had fallen from your shirt to the floor, I knew the restoration of the Sun Stone was at hand. I was overwhelmed with joy. But, that being said, I am very concerned," he said.

"Concerned? Why is that?" I questioned.

"Because Lanier saw the crystal as well." Mur sighed heavily.

I was totally confused.

"Please, Mr. Bunt. It is very important that you understand what your possession of the crystal means."

I sat back in my chair. If only I had a cigar. Or, better still, a bottle of whiskey and a shot glass. Unsure as to the meaning of the crystal, I thought it best to dilute my interest in it. "The crystal? Oh, that old thing? It's something I found lying next to the path as I was traveling from Baratu. I thought it was enchanting, so I picked it up as a souvenir." I said, laughing and feigning indifference.

Mur scowled at my lack of respect. "Mr. Bunt. Please pay attention. There are other scrolls, Mr. Bunt. Many have nothing to do with the Sun Stone, but rather other affairs of our kingdom that have little to do with you. There are four, however, that do involve you. One of the scrolls speaks of the **Chosen One**—one predestined to physically restore the Sun Stone to its full residence.

"Four scrolls? Mur, I'm not blind. There are but three scrolls sitting before you, not four," I corrected.

"Please bear with me, Mr. Bunt. There are few members of the Kingdom who are aware of these scrolls or their contents, and those that do have my devoted confidence.....that is, except for Lanier. Some time ago, while I was away from the palace on a mission for the King, she cast a spell on my guards, causing them to drift into a deep sleep. While they slept, she took all of the scrolls from this chest. When I returned and discovered what she had done, I confronted her, and she returned the scrolls. That is, except the scroll predicting the Chosen One, believing that I would overlook its absence. But I have chosen to never confront her about the missing scroll in order to keep her off guard; not letting on that I know she has it.

"However, she now knows of the Chosen One and poses a serious threat to him and therefore our Kingdom."

"But you still haven't said what this has to do with me," I said, feeling very uncomfortable.

"This first yellow scroll speaks of you, Alan Bunt. Not by name, mind you, but by an action—the action of removing the crystal from the altar in the Cavern of Lights. This scroll speaks of a man who would come to Chandi to save it from extinction by restoring the Sun Stone. The crystal is the key to our Kingdom, and without it, you would never have passed across the bridge of time and space. When you pulled the crystal from the altar, you activated a bridge between your world and ours. You, out of the many who we had hoped would be the one, crossed that bridge and passed through the Door to Chandi. To cement my belief, you brought the blue-eyed Elizabeth with you."

Mur went further. "Every thirteen years, a Leopard Priest is sent to the world you come from in hopes of finding the Chosen One. This priest is allowed thirteen days to find someone he may believe is the Chosen One. Until now, the Chosen One was never found. Certainly, many men were led to the Cavern of Lights, and they, too, were enraptured by the beauty of the crystal. Many tried to remove it, too, but only the Chosen One was able to pull it from its anchor.

"Mr. Bunt, time is short. For once you passed through the waterfall into the Kingdom of Chandi, the clock began to tick. From the time you took the leap of faith through those falls, no more than 13 days may pass before the Sun Stone can be restored."

I couldn't believe what I was hearing.

I chuckled to myself and looked at Mur, "My mentor Dr. Kruger even gave me a piece of rock he believed was part of the Sun Stone, and it fit perfectly in a flaw on its surface."

"Yes," said Mur, "you did have the missing piece in the lagoon. Back in your world. The fact that you had it signaled Chawa that you were special."

"Surely you can't be serious. Chawa abandoned me when the cannibals besieged our camp. If he was to bring me back, why couldn't he have just told me and helped me out. I could have been killed," I chided. "Some Chosen One"

"Chawa was prevented from assisting you, he could offer no help. He is prevented from doing so by instructions contained in the runes. You had to find your way to Chandi on your own. Chawa merely prodded you to that end." Mur said softly, unpreterbed.

"I don't understand. Why couldn't Chawa bring back the missing piece of Sun Stone? He led me right to it and said nothing about it. He knew where it was, why not just bring it home?" I demanded.

"The runes are specific. They prophesied that the Stone will not, and cannot, be restored by anyone other than the Chosen One—one unaware of his destiny, but brave and crafty enough to find it."

"But Mur, why me? I don't belong to this place."

"You must read the scrolls for complete understanding. Do that, and you will be satisfied with the fact that you are the Chosen One and become more focused on your destiny. Of this I am certain."

Mur paused, and without taking his eyes from mine, pushed the three scrolls toward me. "Take your time to completely understand, but know that time is short and we have but a small window of opportunity.

CHAPTER 26

REVELATIONS

I left Mur and found my way back to my quarters as quickly as my feet could carry me. I had the three tightly rolled scrolls tucked securely in my pocket, but I touched them constantly, ensuring that they wouldn't become lost.

Late that night, the jungle became strangely quiet, and the air was heavy and oppressive. I pulled the curtains across the opening to the balcony and extinguished all the torches and candles, except the oil lamp. I brought it to the small table beside my bed and set it in the center. I sat down I opened the first scroll. The yellow one.

It was delicate paper and the writing on it was the most excellent calligraphy, but the years had faded the ink and it was slow reading. Nonetheless, I began.

The Prophesy

On a continent of beauty, where the sun reigns and
the gods are good to men, is a land called Chandi.
The people of this land will establish a nation and thrive.
Its bounty will be plentiful and peace and harmony will
be enjoyed under the watchful eye of its Ruler,
the Sun King.

After one hundred fifty-six cycles of the seasons,
this King shall acquiesce his rule to his first born son,
and that son to his own son, again after
one hundred fifty-six cycles of the seasons.
Thus it shall continue for thirty-nine generations,
the peace of Chandi passed from son to son,

from Sun King to Sun King.
The King who rules this final cycle shall
father four sons, equal in birthright to the throne.
In testimony to this miracle, a great stone shall be
honed from precious jade, a monument proclaiming
the greatness of Chandi and the blessings it is
to receive at the hands of these fours heirs.
From the day of their birth,
fifty-two cycles of the seasons shall pass.
The great Stone will be divided equally
among the pretenders to the throne, a symbol of
each son's equal birthright.
The brothers shall also be divided,
each sent to a distant land to search for destiny.
Count one-hundred four cycles of the seasons,
and the brothers shall be reunited in Chandi,
but with only one destined for kingship.

The Sun Stone shall also be reunited,
symbolizing the enduring strength of the Kingdom.
As long as this Stone remains whole,
Chandi will experience prosperity and peace.
Again, after one hundred fifty-six cycles of the seasons,
this King shall acquiesce his rule, as did his ancestors,
to his first born son, and again
that son to his own son, as before.
Thus it shall continue again for thirty-nine generations,
the peace of Chandi passed from son to son,

ALAN BUNT & THE PROPHESY

from Sun King to Sun King.
But woe to those who live during the dark days,
when the earth shall shake and the peace be shattered.
For the King of the seventy-eighth generation
shall betray Chandi to one from a faraway land,
Beware of her who is of great beauty,
whose eyes are blue like
the sky and whose skin is as soft as the clouds.

She shall hypnotize his heart and
numb his judgment to satisfy her evil and selfish heart.
Woe to those who live during the dark days,
when the blue-eyed one shall separate
from the great Stone one portion, the Spirit, and hide it.
During those days, a black cloud shall
appear on the horizon, blotting the sun from every eye.
The land shall suffer, and the spirit of the people will fade.
The King will rule, but as the voice of the blue-eyed one.
She shall seek to rule Chandi with a scepter of iron forever.
She shall seek allegiance of the people but gain it not.
She shall plot to kill the firstborn son of the King,
hoping to end the bloodline.
She shall fail.

Woe to those who live during the dark days,
for the holy sage of Chandi shall use
his might to oppose the blue-eyed one,
The one who will endeavor to

keep the great Stone incomplete,
forever sealing the fate of Chandi to be
a land without a heart, without a spirit.

The Holy One shall bear her wrath for the people
Until the time of Shandru,
who shall return after one-hundred fifty-six cycles
of the seasons, delivering his people from her grip
and saving Chandi from extinction.

I was sweating profusely. Even though my trembling hands made it somewhat difficult, I reread the scroll, making sure that what I was reading was really on the page. There was no mistaking that Mur was the holy sage, but who was the Shandru? What was the Shandru? And what about the blue-eyed one? I rolled the scroll up, secured it tightly with the golden braid and set it to one side. I paused for a brief moment to gather my wits. I took the green scroll and untied the band.

CHAPTER 27

THE SHANDRU

This scroll was in worse shape than the others. Its sides were ragged and a corner of the parchment was torn off, cutting off the ends of a few of the last sentences. As I unrolled it, small fragments fell from its edges. As with the first scroll, the ink was faded and was difficult to read. Also, the script was in an entirely different hand, and it took me a few moments to familiarize myself with the style.

Immediately, I saw that one of my questions was about to be answered.

The One Who Is To Come

It is written that a dark cloud
Shall envelope the Crater of Tan,
Hiding it from the eyes of the world,
Exorcised from the memory of man.

The pangs of royal childbirth shall echo
Over the valley as the armies of the betrayer
Prepare for battle, sharpening their swords to
The impatient cries of the Cathartidae.

The thundering hooves of the enemy approach,
the stink of death draws near.
The appointed, the Chawa, in service to the Holy One
Shall take the child to his breast and flee,
separating the Spirit, the Shandru,

From the land and the Sting of the Blue-eyed one.
The earth shall tremble, the mountains shall heave and sigh
And time will cease as the war for the soul of Chandi rages.
After a while, death will be sated and the blue-eyed one
Shall subdue the King and exert power over him.

The space of one hundred fifty-six seasons
shall pass in the netherworld,
And the King, father of the Shandru,
bows before the blue-eyed one.
The Holy One of Chandi, Keeper of the Secret Curse, shall send forth the Chawa, The Appointed, to search for Hope, the Spirit of Chandi. The One who is to Come.

This Chosen One, the Shandru, will be ignorant of his heritage;
he comes in the guise of a mortal,
with queen so fair and eyes of blue.
With this he brings uneasiness and doubt, for in the kingdom two beautiful ones reside, both with the eyes of the color of the blue skies and from faraway lands.
On the shoulders of this man,
the Holy One of Chandi shall place
Chandi's fate in its rightful Kingdom and Domain.

On the Shandru will be bestowed the power
of the sacred leopard,
The heart of the lion, the wile of the panther.
He shall slay the blue eyed Deceiver,

And rescue the heart of the King. He shall make whole the
mighty Stone and with it the Spirit of Chandi shall return.

After the Shandru reestablishes the soul of Chandi
He shall rule for but a small time, For his heart will yearn
For the land from whence he came and he shall return,
To live his final days, sealing Chandi from him forever.

But from his seed another king shall emerge, This one shall
Return to the Golden Land to establish a new kingdom,
the new Chandi.
He shall bequeath to the land Four Treasures
that will cause the
New kingdom to be mighty and prosperous.

The first shall be a great wall to stop the sacred waters
For the benefit of the land and all who live in it.
The waters that nurture the earth will be captive
And quench the thirst for all living things.

The second shall be the establishment of wildlife long missing,
To again walk the earth and live together in natural bliss.
The lion and the kudu shall coexist as brothers and
The birds of the sky find refuge in the trees.

Mighty and great shall be the new land,
For the Third Treasure opens the new Chandi
To the world, to cause it to share its bounty and

Prosperity with those in the far reaches of the world.
Lastly, the progeny of the last Sun King
Shall return to the new Kingdom from the four corners
Of the world, to live and work ever diligently, to build a great
Palace in the new Kingdom as a beacon to the world.

So it will be!

I stared at the scroll, troubled. I reached up and rubbed my eyes. They ached and felt dry, as if I had been staring into nothingness for quite some time. I was now convinced that I have stumbled into some kind of time labyrinth. I blinked and looked at the candle. It had melted to a tiny pool of paraffin, and the flame danced from the snake-like wick. I felt suspended in time and, for a moment, I couldn't feel my legs. My shadow loomed large on the wall.

Again, I looked at the scroll, ruminating on its contents, its significance. Of one thing I was sure, I felt concern about for this Shandru character, quite a chore he had before him. That is, if he existed.

Only one thing kept troubling me. If Lainer really was the Blue-eyed one, she existed! But. I definitely refused to bring Elizabeth into the whole picture, for you see she was also blue-eyed!

I decided to surrender to this surreal state. I chuckled to myself. Alan, I thought, remember the term "gullible?" I rolled up the scroll and placed it next to the first scroll.

Dare I read the third?

CHAPTER 28

THE QUICKENING

Before I unrolled the last scroll, I stopped to consider what I had learned. If I read correctly, it seems that Chandi is to have a war and lose. Or perhaps the war had already been fought, sometime in the past. Strange, I thought, no one said a thing to me about any war. As a matter of fact, things seem pretty peaceful around here. Inzer had said nothing about a war. And surely I would have read about it somewhere.

And this Shandru fellow. Surely Inzer would have said something about him. Maybe he doesn't even know about him. Mur did say that only he and Lanier had seen these scrolls, but had either divulged the contents to the citizens? That I couldn't determine.

The more things focused, the more they blurred, hidden from understanding. It was a strange feeling, as I usually pride myself in putting two and two together. I felt lost, yet curious beyond control.

I took a deep breath and snapped my attention back to the third scroll before me and carefully spread it out on the table.

The Quickening

Do not despair, O lonely Chandi. Provision for hope lies beyond your secret boundaries. Though you be dead, devoid of spirit, there is cause to rejoice, for you shall live once again, the Spirit returned by the Shandru and The Great Stone reunited, though the Blue-eyed one will seek to slay him and endeavor to keep The Great Stone dispersed. But the Shandru will prevail and Chandi will begin anew, cradled in the arms of peace and prosperity, once the Holy One of Chandi shall lift his curse over the land. Then will the Shandru stand tall, with his queen beside him, to oversee the resurrection of Chandi and the restoration of the Palace. His birthright place.

I rubbed my eyes. By now, I really was tired. It seemed as if I had been reading these scrolls for the longest time, yet there were only three. Sorting all of this out was going to take some time and I was not in any condition to do so right now. My eyes grew heavy and soon drowsiness overtook my racing mind, and lulled it into sleep. I fell into oblivion.

CHAPTER 29

THE BROKEN SECRET

I lay staring at the ceiling as the new day's sun peeked over the horizon. I couldn't shake the feeling of impending doom. I hoped it was just my tired body telling me that it needed rest, but my mind was so intensely fixed on the stories I found in the scrolls that it ignored my weariness and delighted in taunting my reason and intellect. Such incredible things were written.

A zephyr of fresh air wafted through the opening of the patio and helped to cast off a few of the cobwebs that detained me in my stupor. I sat up and swung my legs to the side of the bed and stared at the three scrolls on the table, tightly twisted into tubes and secured by the golden cords. Suddenly I became worried, wondering about my fate should I be caught with these scrolls. I didn't know whom to trust at this point. I gathered up the scrolls and hid them under the pile of pillows that decorated one of the rooms' corners.

I left my room heading for nowhere in particular. I needed solitude, for sure, but I felt trapped in that room. I needed space to breathe and to sort out this whole troubling episode. I prayed no one would interrupt my aloneness; I wouldn't know how to react. I must have wandered aimlessly for hours, for midmorning I found myself seated at the foot of the stairs at the Old East Gate. I was lost in thought when someone's presence startled me.

Behind me, and alone, the Sun King himself came down the stairs, slowly and obviously preoccupied. To my surprise, he sat down right next to me and addressed me as if he had known me for years.

"Why so deep in thought? Are you troubled?" he asked. "Perhaps you haven't eaten. It is not a good thing to be so concerned on an empty stomach."

I did my best to conduct myself with some semblance of protocol. I deflected the urge to be self-indulgent.

"I pray, kind Sire, that my wanderings has not disturbed you or interrupted your activities this morning," I blathered foolishly.

Then another odd occurrence happened, he put his arm on my shoulder. "Actually, you seem so aloof, as if the weight of the world is burdening you. Your mind finds no peace because your heart is heavy with confusion," he said.

His observation brought a weak smile to my face. He was correct, of course. But though I was searching for answers, I didn't dare impose on him.

"I wish there was something I could do to ease your load," he said sincerely. "Let me tell you a story. Perhaps you will see that even the powerful men, those with the world at their beck and call, become encumbered with regrets and the clutter of bad decisions, your own discomposure might be eased and your equanimity restored. Fear not the affliction of your soul, for even at the darkest hour the promise of a new day is ours."

I nodded. Already I felt a bit better, but probably because I was so enraptured that His Highness was even here, beside me. Even so, the words spoken by his deep, calming voice was soothing and provided a small measure of much needed balm.

"I'd like to hear it, Great One. Tell me your story and I shall be forever in your debt," I said.

"So be it. Listen carefully, for some day it may be of help to you," he said.

I nodded again and he began.

"Our present is our past. It was during the Jackal's Era of Chandi, about one hundred fifty six seasons ago, that strange people arrived from the great Sea of the South. It was on our southern border that they established a village. As nature saw fit, they soon began to live among the people of Chandi. And though they shared much knowledge and seemed, for the most part, to be a peaceful lot, they experienced much dissent and division among themselves, causing trouble among the native people of this valley.

"Mur, High Priest and Counselor of our land, was very sensitive to any imbalance in our Kingdom, immediately perceived trouble for the King and his people."

"Mur knew that the time had come for a prophecy to be fulfilled. He warned the Sun King and begged him to exile the foreigners from Chandi."

The more the King talked, the more I wallowed in confusion. Was he speaking of himself as King, or had it been another before him? I wondered.

The Sun King, if aware of my confusion, paid no heed but continued with the story. "But the King was an unhappy ruler. Though he had a queen, his first wife; one he liked and found amusing, he cared little in his heart for her. However, he carefully hid his dissatisfaction from her, as she was pregnant with his child. His unhappiness was overwhelming, and his quiet, internal battle to gain personal felicity consumed him. Consequently, the King treated Mur's warning as mere folly, as predicted. Mur's counsel fell on deaf ears, as the foolish King, mighty and powerful, was already under the hypnotic spell of one as beautiful as she was dangerous, a princess of royal blood, a daughter to the visiting king from the Southlands. Her name was Reinal. She possessed a beauty that escaped most women: deep, steel-blue eyes against perfect, milky-white skin that contrasted sharply with her long, black, shiny hair. She maintained a charming personality and was quick in thought and intelligence. But she did have a serious flaw: an ambition that could never be satisfied.

"One day, just prior to the calamity, the King left his Palace to visit the southern part of Chandi and to visit the new people and share in some important festivities, as good neighbors should do. It didn't take long for the lonely Sun King to fall prey to the hypnotic beauty and charm of Reinal. It wasn't long before the captivated King asked her to marry him.

"Reinal responded even quicker. 'Nothing would make me happier than accepting your marriage proposal.' What she said next was most troubling, yet did little to dissuade the King from retracting his proposal.

"Since I was very young," Reinal said matter-of-factly," I have always desired to rule a beautiful Kingdom; not as the daughter of a powerful King, but as a queen, equal to my husband, having dominion over a prosperous Kingdom and its peace-loving people. I feel greatly honored, Your Grace, and accept your proposal...with one condition: you must promise that no secret, however small, shall ever exist between us."

"The Sun King swore this oath: 'I swear on my life that from this day on I freely place my life into your hands. I promise that nothing shall ever come between you and I, and that nothing be confided to my heart that be not confided in you."

"Not many seasons passed since their betrothal when the Sun King, blinded by love and trapped by passion, confided to his second wife Chandi's most precious secret: the secret of the Kingdom's prosperity and peaceful existence. The King betrayed Chandi by disclosing that Chandi's success lay in the Great Sun Stone—that as long the four quarters of the stone touched, no nation could subdue and oppress Chandi. But beware should the Stone be separated, since the power of the Sun Stone would then be diminished and the Kingdom would be vulnerable to all sorts of evils.

"Early the next morning, after a night of quiet calculation, the traitorous princess secretly visited the chambers of her father. She told her father that she had discovered the secret of the Sun King's power and invincibility of Chandi's existence and how it could be overcome. Her father, himself a greedy, dark-hearted

THE TWO GUARDS

man, begged her to reveal the secret to him. She agreed, but only with the condition that her father, upon conquering the Sun King, was to proclaim her queen and the sole, absolute ruler of Chandi, including the impressive Palace and its treasures, and lord over the people. She was, however, willing to share with her father the fabulous wealth of the mines—reservoirs of gems and precious metals so extensive that there was more than enough for both of them.

"Once Reinal's father agreed to her demand, she told her father the secret. The foreign king immediately sent his best four warriors to steal and destroy the four portions of the Great Sun Stone, neutralizing the self-sustaining power of the Valley of Chandi.

"The very next day, after realizing his error and betrayal, the Sun King urgently summoned Mur. He was heartbroken that he had divulged the secret of Chandi and begged the old wizard for advice.

Sadly, Mur shook his head and told him, "For what you have done to all of us in the name of love, we must all pay. The only way we can save our beautiful kingdom is to suspend it in time; that is, to stop time. Only then can we prepare to fight back, fueled by the hope of deliverance by the promised Shandru."

My ears immediately perked up even more and I blinked, and choked back any poorly-thought-out remarks about the Shandru.

The King continued, apparently not noticing my reaction.

Mur declared "As for you, Sun King, you shall live a life full of remorse, grieving each day deliverance is delayed. But worry not, as for your dynasty shall prevail in the end. For the Shandru will come indeed, one who has your blood coursing through his veins. The dynasty will continue. And though Chandi will be locked in a suspension of time, it will survive. But for now, you must suffer, if only to fully understand the magnitude of what you have just done to all of us. Divulging Chandi's sacred secret will bring consequences, and you shall be witness to them, as will all of your subjects. We will all pay dearly, but we all shall have hope."

Mur then bowed and turned away from the King.

"What's next? Where are you off to?" inquired the distressed King.

Mur sighed and, in deference to his Highness, told him, "It is imperative that I withdraw to the Cavern immediately and tend to safety of the Great Stone before our enemies discover you have told me of your indiscretion. If I don't, terrible things will begin to happen."

"Mur wasted little time with court etiquette, as he turned and left the sorrowful King to wallow in his remorse and unhappiness. Mur briskly made his way to the

Cavern and the Temple of Rajun, followed closely by the Leopard High Priests and their twin guardians. By this time, all of them were aware of the terrible prospect. If only they could protect the Stone.

"They were too late. As they neared the secret entrance to the Cavern, they discovered four enemy soldiers had found it, and were fervently working to remove part of the Great Stone.

"Mur wasted little time and invoked a spell, causing the Spirits to become violently angry.

"Unbeknown to Mur, the Queen had given birth to a baby boy, the first born of the Sun King and pretender to the Throne. In the throes of childbirth, the Queen died and the small baby was immediately wrapped in some cloths and whisked away by the Chawa, the appointed of Mur. This Chawa had been instructed by Mur to save the heir to the Throne of Chandi, even with the cost of his own life if necessary. As he left the palace, Mur had just invoked his spell.

"At that moment, a terrible explosion shook the entire valley. Lur, the sleeping volcano, had been awakened after years of peaceful sleep. Earthquakes followed and punished the land. The whole Kingdom rocked back and forth. The people ran, full of panic, with no escape. Animals randomly scattered everywhere, the roars of the panthers and the shrieking of the monkeys were deafening.

"Back at the Cavern entrance, Mur turned and looked over the entire Valley, the Crater of Tan.

"With his heart heavy and full of sorrow, Mur lifted his arms and hands to the sky and implored, 'By the Power of the Sun Stone, given to us by you, Mighty Protector, have mercy on your people, embrace your Kingdom and wrap us in the safety of your presence. Cease time as it is and everything in it."

As the ground shook, the enemy soldiers managed to separate one quarter of the Great Stone from its mates. They made their way down to the side of the great monolith and disappeared through another exit from the Cavern. The guards at the door to the bridge became so frightened that they deserted their posts and headed back to the palace. It was then that they were approached by the Chawa, who ran past them so quickly that they seemed to pause, as if to determine what was happening. They then recognized the Chawa, and started after him. They were held off by the Chawa's Leopard-twin for a brief time, but managed to kill it and continue their pursuit of the Chawa unaware of his precious cargo.

"The Chawa raced to the entrance of the cavern and made his way across the stone bridge that connected to the great altar of the Sun Stone in the Temple of

REINAL'S SPELL

Rajun. As he disappeared through the entrance, the ground shook even more, hindering the chase by the soldiers. They threw their spears at him, but it is unknown if he was hit. That was the last time **the Chawa and the child were ever seen.**

"In the meantime, the volcano exploded and Mur continued his incantation, provoking the spirits and causing a great wind and fury to roar through the land. the people screamed and begged for mercy, yet the onslaught intensified.

"Mur, in one last effort, raised his hands to the heavens and implored the great Sun God for mercy.

"In that moment and with a terrible and violent explosion, Chandi disappeared from the face of the earth—the Palace, its people, the animals—and along with it, the earth's memory of the Kingdom of Chandi was erased. Only Chandi wasn't destroyed—it only seemed to cease ***to EXIST."***

CHAPTER 30

THE CHOSEN ONE

I sat still, unable to move My mind reeled at this most incredible story.

"I'm not sure that you realize it, Mr. Bunt, but Chandi is under this spell even as I speak. Our separation from the world will continue until the return of the Shandru, The Chosen One. Only he can cast the curse from our midst."

"The Chosen One" I mumbled aloud, remembering Mur's reference to this elusive character. "I thought that he was just a character in a fairy tale; a figment of some wild imagination."

"On the contrary," protested the King. "The Shandru is very much alive and has entered into our midst."

He looked directly into my eyes. "You, Alan Bunt, are the Chosen One."

This can't be happening, I thought to myself. At that moment, I sat, frozen in silence, searching for understanding. I decided to again deflect any attention centered on me.

"Me?" I scoffed, "Surely you have the wrong man. I'm certainly no hero. Besides, I grew up in England, in a small village where my mother lives to this day."

My rationale gave me a dose of reality, so my churning insides calmed down considerably, grasping out of this madness something that invalidated the King's outrageous claim.

The King just shook his head, and chuckled to himself. Obviously, there was nothing I could do to stifle this silliness. The good King's serene confidence contrasted sharply with my growing uneasiness.

"How do I know you are the Shandru, the Chosen One? It's very simple," he said dryly. "Open up the pocket of your shirt, Mr. Bunt. It is prophesied that the Chosen One will possess the key to the gate of Chandi. The key is the crystal, plucked from the axis of the Great Stone—the divided Stone. And you, Mr. Bunt, have that crystal. We all saw it at the grand feast, when it fell from your clothing. You are the Chosen One."

The old King stood and arched his back, stretching and swaying. He bent over and offered me his hand. I looked at him to find his eyes welled up with tears. I took his hand and he pulled me to my feet. Then, to my sudden shock, he wrapped his arms around me and hugged me so hard I got lightheaded.

He then held me at arms length and said, "Many, many seasons have passed, when the Chawa rescued you from certain death the very day you were born. He took you from our Kingdom to safety in what is now the outside world. When that Chawa, that leopard priest, gave his life to see you to safety, he saved Chandi in the process: from Reinal and her father. You see, Mur cast the spell to protect Chandi by suspending it in time until the Shandru returned thirty-nine years later to restore the Sun Stone, and bring spirit and prosperity back. Because we are suspended in time, we neither have the power of the Stone nor have we lost it. This keeps Reinal and her father powerless, since none in the land have power—as it really doesn't exist...for the time being. But in the outside world, time does exist, and after thirty-nine years, the age of ascension to the Chandian throne, the small infant will have grown to fulfill his destiny: to return to Chandi through no planning of his own accord, to restore the Sun Stone and take his rightful place as Lord over the people."

"Wait, wait, wait," I stopped the King. "There's something wrong here. If, as you say, I am this so-called Chosen One, the Shandru I believe he's named, and I am to save your Sun Stone and this Kingdom, and then, as some grand finale, prance right in and claim this throne you speak of, that means you're my father. And as I said, I grew up in England. It's just not possible."

"Yes!" he shout. "You, Alan Bunt, are the baby that was saved that day of darkness and despair. You are the Shandru. You are **my son returned to save us all."**

I noticed my hands were moist and I was dripping with perspiration. My stomach wrenched with nausea, and I leaned against one of the columns to stabilize my vertigo. Surely this can't be, I said to myself again and again.

By now, we weren't alone. Three Leopard High Priests had gathered near. I felt a bit trapped! Then the King's tone changed.

"Quickly now," he ordered with an acute urgency. "The Chosen One must be ordained at sundown."

He grasped me by the elbow and propelled me towards the Palace.

My mind raced. Ordained? I'm not being ordained because this isn't really happening.

The Leopard High Priests followed in silence. The afternoon sun flickered off the pointed, shiny, bronze tusks of the colossal elephant sculpture. It seemed as if a river of fire slowly flowed along their long curves.

Splendid. Just splendid, I murmured to myself sarcastically. I'm sure they all believed I had finally accepted the idea of my importance, in spite of my protestations. At the far horizon, I saw the sun's reflections, in golden tones, kiss the surface of Chandi's lagoon. The afternoon shadows grew long with the aging of another day. When we reached the bottom of the Royal Staircase, a flourish of fanfares announced our arrival. My escort led me to the top of the stairs, and we were immediately met by a ceremonial committee, lavishly clothed and ornamented. For a moment, everything stood still under the archway of the majestic East Gate. The whole picture was impressive. It was obviously an important moment to all, although I still wasn't totally convinced I should acknowledge it by becoming a willing participant. I inhaled deeply. It seemed as if the entire population of Chandi had gathered under the archway to stand motionless, eyes fixed on me. I felt light in the head, and eerie feeling that I was suspended in....suspended in time!

The twelve Leopard High Priests, each with their leopard-twin following, advanced toward where I stood, unable to move due to fear and anticipation. As they got within touching distance, with an almost imperceptible hand movement by one of the Priests, two fair maidens emerged from the crowd and came to me. Each took one of my hands without saying a word. In silence, they led me to the main fountain, and waded in, pulling me in behind them. They then had me stand in its center. In the blink of an eye, they completely undressed me. I tried to cover myself, but I failed to achieve any sense of modesty. Then, against my protests, the young girls began to bathe me, with great care, with golden water of the fountain. I was shielded from the others by the bodies of the girls. One faced me; the other behind me. I must confess that after a brief while, the shame I felt at my nudity disappeared. The girls began rubbing my body with warm and fragrant oils, causing my skin to tingle. After drying and oiling my feet, soft, skin sandals were placed on my feet. These soft sandals covered my ankles with a peculiar ornamentation. I was beckoned to stand. The taller of the two girls then shrouded my body with an incredible suit of leopard skin. It fit so tightly, and it felt like a second skin. On my right hand, they placed a glove that had the sharpest claws protruding from the ends of the fingers. It wasn't long until I discovered that I could make it move just by thinking about it!

As they dressed me, I felt as if I were being transformed into something ghastly, something bridging the difference between man and animal. My feelings of mortality diminished with every passing moment. It was as if I had become one of the leopards that sat quietly around the fountain. As these sensations and transforma-

THE SHANDRU

tions continued, two High Priests placed a cape over my shoulders, a cape of elephant and rhinoceros skins. Again, I felt a peculiar animal instinct rise within me. At the same time, I felt liberated and at ease, and the fear I harbored began to ebb. In my left hand was placed a bag of spicy herbs. I slung the bag over my shoulder, as if I had done this before.

Then the two Leopard High Priests completely submerged me in the gold water of the fountain. The overflow of the fountain pool descended rapidly down the central channel carved in the Royal Stairs. The dying sun disappeared behind the thin line of the horizon. Extraordinary as it may sound, at the exact moment the first golden drop reached the bottom of the Royal Stairs, the last streak of sunlight blinked good-bye. The High Priests helped me stand, and as they did so, a powerful ray began ascending the Royal Stairway's central channel. It rose slowly, illuminating the stairs. It reached me, still standing, shivering, in the pool and entwined my body, producing a pulsating, luminescent glow.

As the glowing energy surged through me, I thought of the scrolls and all that I had read about and what I had been told. Chandi was becoming part of me, and I a part of Chandi. Then, as quickly as it had arrived, the strange ray vanished. One of the High Priests turned to the crowd and raised his arms to the sky and shouted, "It has been accomplished!"

Reality suddenly overwhelmed me. I blinked my eyes, and the torches came into focus. Their dancing light flickered and played across the terrace. I was led back to the Palace, to the Kudu's Tower, the highest tower, for a night of meditation and preparation. (Oddly, I had attempted to enter this tower, without invitation, several times since my arrival, and had always been refused entry.) The room at the top of the tower was circular, and the walls were completely covered with scrolls and shelves and shelves of some of the oldest books I had ever seen. In the center of the room rose an altar made of stone, a replica of the altar in the cavern at the Temple of Rajun. In its center, a small model of the restored Sun Stone, lay flat, as had the incomplete Stone I had seen only days before. But with this altar, instead of marking its center with a magnificent crystal like the one I still had, it was marked with an indentation from which a flame quivered, illuminating the room with a warm glow.

Silently, each Leopard High Priest that had accompanied me to the Kudu's Tower took a bow before the altar stone and left. As the last one made his way to the door, he turned and nodded farewell. The sound of the closing door caused a rush of excitement within me. What came next? What was expected of me now?

My body had had enough. I collapsed on the bed and quickly faded into sleep. It was a short sleep, but sound, as I awoke a few hours later to the black of night, refreshed and alert. I walked to the window and looked out into the darkness—a darkness I suspected held even more secrets than I could imagine. A longing pierced my spirit and a peculiar sensation flooded through my body, a feeling that "something" or "someone" took possession of my body, which I no longer controlled.

I became restless, and began to pace, like a caged animal. When the night's odors wafted through the open window, I impulsively went to the door and opened it, and carefully looked out to see if there were any guards. Seeing none, I bounded down the stairs into the freedom of the night.

I walked for a while (or was I prowling?), and my new sandals shuffled over the moist earth. Before long, a familiar scent captured my attention. I followed my nose and eventually I found myself lurking in the gardens that surrounded the Princesses' wing of the Palace. An uneasiness surged through me, my intuition alerting me that I shouldn't be there. As I turned to bound into the darkness, Elizabeth came out onto her balcony. Although she appeared tired and drawn, she was an incredible sight and a great relief to me. Her glorious mane of blonde curls were beautifully disarrayed, her night dress wrinkled. She scanned the starry skies and heaved a sigh fraught with longing. As she studied the night sky, I watched her quietly. I wanted to jump out, to yell "Hello," and rush to her arms. But I stayed put, cautious of the uneasiness I felt.

Elizabeth leaned on the edge of the balcony and looked out. I'm sure she looked right at me, but she apparently couldn't see me as there was no response.

Then she appeared to again focus in my direction and leaned into the darkness. She paused for a long while, and then, to my great surprise, she whispered into the night, "Alan? Is that you?"

When Elizabeth called my name, my heart leapt and I immediately stepped out into the open. Elizabeth's face turned white, and she recoiled the moment she laid eyes on me.

"Who are you?" she asked, sounding afraid.

It was then I remembered that I was still in the leopard cape and ceremonial

ELIZABETH AT THE BALCONY

attire. I tried to speak to her, but when I tried, a horrible roar jumped from my throat—one that scared even me.

She stepped back, her eyes black with fear. She couldn't recognize me and I couldn't talk.

"Stay away from me!" She cried, as I moved towards her.

I moved slowly, cautiously feline, never taking my eyes off her. As I approached the balcony from below, her fear overwhelmed her and she turned and ran into her room, pulling the curtains closed behind her, as if they offered protection.

Why had I continued walking towards her, when it was obvious I couldn't explain anything to her, I wasn't sure. Maybe I wanted to erase the fear Elizabeth's face carried. Maybe I just wanted to hold her. When she fled in panic to her room, I heard a short gasp and the sounds of a violent struggle.

"Help, help me!"

Her frightened voice was barely audible, even with my new cat ears.

I reacted with the suddenness of lightning. I ran as fast as I could towards her voice and in one single jump I reached her balcony only to see a terrified Elizabeth being restrained by two tall guards.

"Leave me alone! Sun King shall hear about this!" She screamed at the two soldiers, all the time trying to free herself from their grasp.

I saw they had no intention of setting her free, so I pounced out of the darkness into the room. Both men, totally surprised by my unexpected arrival, let go of Elizabeth and fell backwards. I shook my head, roared menacingly, and I started walking slowly towards the guards. I roared again. I don't believe even a second passed before they ran outside, jumped off the balcony, and disappear into the jungle below.

Elizabeth slumped in the corner, badly shaken and terrorized. She tried to make herself small, invisible, and it was obvious from her shaking that she was equally frightened of me. I knew she hadn't recognized me, but I was sure if I could get her to touch me, she would stop being afraid. So I extended my right hand, silently asking for hers.

For the longest time she just stared at me. Finally, she placed her trembling hand in mine. I helped her up to her feet. As the seconds flew by, we didn't move, our eyes locked, searching for a connection. Elizabeth looked deep into my eyes, looking for a hint as to who, or what, I was. I could sense her confusion, torn between fear and trust, but I could not speak, and so, with much longing, I released her hand. She took a small step back. Without a word, I moved to the window and grabbed a sturdy vine growing up the side of the balcony and descended to the ground below.

I returned to the High Tower, but sleep eluded me. What in heaven's name has happened to me? Despite my new attire why hadn't Elizabeth recognized me? Why was I roaring instead of speaking?

I crossed the tower room to the basin of water sitting on the table. I reached down for a drink and was frightened by my reflection in the water. True, there remained a faint resemblance to Alan Bunt, but I was more beast than human. My body had transformed to resemble an erect leopard and my face definitely had feline characteristics. Even my size was not quite the same anymore. Indeed, I had gone through an extraordinary transformation. No wonder Elizabeth hadn't recognized me. I couldn't even recognize myself —not the way I looked now.

Again, I found myself pacing about the room. Finally, my body just gave out and sleep made a welcome visit.

I was awakened by two Leopard High Priests who had placed a plate of food on the table. It smelled delicious. I inspected the food—kudu meat and water—and it tasted good.

A good many hours had gone by, and still, I found myself asking, "Why me?"

I walked to the open window and looked to the sky. I couldn't answer any of my own questions about this predicament in which I found myself, but I faced up to one thing, I knew my life had changed and somehow my control over it had vanished.

CHAPTER 31

MUR AND THE HERO "SHANDRU"

I woke with a deep feeling of anticipation. Anxiety still gnawed at me, and I continued to pace the room, back and forth, to and fro. It would be impossible to relate everything that passed through my mind. While I was still unsure of what had happened to me, surprisingly with every step I was feeling a sense of surging strength. My muscles tensed automatically when I heard a knock at the door.

Mur entered the room. I had not seen him since he had given me the scrolls. He eyed me carefully, and then said matter-of-factly, "Your time has come, Shandru."

I walked to the open window and took a deep breath. With my back to Mur, I stretched my arms upwards, arching my body. "Mur, you must help me. Although I now understand many things about the Kingdom of Chandi, I feel unsure of what is required of me. And these changes that have occurred in me, with my body, with my senses, give me a feeling I have never experienced."

Mur muttered to himself impatiently. "Mortal men are always full of questions."

"Mur, I now understand that I am the Shandru and that I am to restore the Sun Stone to complete the Kingdom of Chandi. But what has this to do with the changes that have happened to me? Am I to always be this way? Forever?" I asked.

Mur avoided the answer and instead asked me to calm down and have a seat.

"Allow me, Shandru, to fill in a few of the empty spaces," he offered.

"I am Mur. I am not only a magician, as you rightly call me, but a High Priest also. I am a spirit that will live eternally....in this world. I don't belong to any particular time. I simply exist—from the beginning until now and through the end of time.

"The time of the world from which you come and time in Chandi are not the same, as you have surely already perceived. Our dimension is not the same, either. We exist apart from your world, though there is a connecting bridge between both. I understand its difficult for you to accept but the truth is it exists. Destiny has led you here. It was preordained that you would find your way here and assume your role as the 'Chosen One.'

"I already revealed to you, through the scrolls, the prophecies that pertain to Chandi and to the Chosen One. You now know our past, our present and future. When you are as old as I, perhaps you'll realize our calling is not always as clear as we would like, or that it is what we would like it to be."

"It is true that the time of restoration will come during the reign of a King with four daughters. As you know, this reign is now underway. It is also true that restoration of the Great Stone cannot take place until the King has his heart in the grasp of a beautiful, blue-eyed woman. I know that you have experienced the icy, lifeless stare of Lanier, the blue-eyed temptress that now controls the heart of our beloved king. The people of Chandi have been tricked into believing that she is the Queen about whom the runes speak. But I know that Lanier is not the one," Mur elaborated. "The prophecies speak of a blue-eyed queen who has a heart of love and respect for our people. Lanier is evil and has a heart blackened with contempt and jealousy."

"So, if she is not the one, then the time of restoration is not at hand." I paused. "I'm terribly sorry. I know that it is a big disappointment. And that probably means that I am not the Shandru!" I said, momentarily quite relieved.

"Not so," Mur said quickly. "The blue-eyed one is here. You brought her to us. It is Elizabeth."

My heart contracted. "Elizabeth? Certainly you can't be serious. She is just an innocent victim of circumstance. Had we not shared a frightening experience with some pretty dangerous characters, man-eaters, I might add, we would not have even met. It was pure chance that our paths crossed."

"Destiny has no reason, Shandru. And I am not one to question the reasons why you were thrown together. All I know, and accept, is the fact that you are both here, now in this important time in Chandi's history. And as far as your encounter with the evil cannibals in your world, it will not be as frightening as an encounter with Lanier in our world. Lanier knows that she, herself, is not the blue-eyed one spoken of in the runes and she will do anything in her power to stop the Shandru and the rightful blue-eyed one from ever fulfilling the prophecies. And the key to that end is to prevent the Sun Stone from being restored. The holy Stone's division is how she is able to retain her power over the Sun King and the Kingdom. And, Shandru, Lanier is the reason that I ordered Elizabeth to be separated from you, so that she, the true blue-eyed mistress of our Kingdom, would be out of harm's way, away from the claws of Lanier, who would destroy her, and you, in an instant.

"Where is Lanier now?" I asked, now knowing her danger to Elizabeth.

"She's hiding with her own brand of magic. She disappeared almost immediately after she saw that you were in possession of the green crystal. I'm not quite sure to where she withdrew, or if she merely changed identity, but I'm sure she's close enough to fully understand that her days are numbered." Mur seemed quite concerned by this time.

I quickly gathered my senses and asked, "What about your magic, Mur? Can't you do something?"

He shook his head. "Although I'm powerful, I'm not infallible. My magic is useless when it comes to fulfillment of prophecy. My magic would only hinder the course of events, delay them, perhaps even change the predicted outcome. And I don't want that.

"That is why you are now here," Mur said, pointing his finger at me. "You. The Shandru. The Chosen One!"

For the first time, and much to my amazement, he spoke with great deference and respect for me, and bowed very low.

At that moment, the new spirit within me began to speak with great confidence and authority. "All right, Mur. Chandi has had her long wait, but here I am. The question is, when am I to undertake this great deed. How much longer until my quest begins?"

"Today," he exclaimed. "The time is now."

That was not the answer I had hoped for, but it was one I could deal with.

"Then, Mur, please tell me where I am to begin. And how?"

"Do you remember the Sun Stone? The one you and Chawa discovered in the lagoon?" he asked, surely knowing the answer.

"Yes!

"Your task is to bring it back and restore it to the other three stones that lie on the altar in the Temple of Rajun, in the great cavern. It was stolen by the foot soldiers of Lanier's and her father's army the very day you were taken from Chandi by the Chawa. We are fortunate that they absconded with only the one piece, as this will make your quest easier...if that is possible. It is our dearest desire, since Chandi's ultimate power and strength lies in the reunification of those four stones.

"Remember, Lanier is a witch, a powerful witch and can and will use all of her power to see that the stone remains broken apart. But I know you offer the most promising chance for it to become whole again, and I, representing all of Chandi, throw myself at the feet of your good mercy." Again, he bowed low, making me very uncomfortable.

I paced the room in silence, pondering the situation. Our situation, thinking of Elizabeth.

"Mur." I looked at him directly in the eyes. "Should I accept this challenge that is apparently set for none other but me, will Elizabeth and I be free to go after its completion? That is, should I succeed?"

"Yes," nodded Mur. "Yes, you will be free to return to the outer world, with our most sincere blessings and gratitude."

Mur was staring at me, and deep in his eyes flickered the flame of hope.

"Should I succeed, no more ties or promises?" I wanted to be sure.

"Only those which you take upon yourself. You have my word," he said. I believed him.

"One final question, Mur. In the event, or if by any happening, I lose my life in this adventure while saving your 'nonexistent' Kingdom, can your magic restore me back to life in my own world?" At that moment, I realized that this was an unfair question, because it seems that destiny was going to lead me where it will. I began to retract it, but Mur was quick to answer.

"I'm afraid not, Shandru. Death is final—here and there."

A heavy silence screamed in my ears. Again, I paced. I felt like a trapped animal, studying the same confines over and over.

"Please settle down, Shandru. Time is short and you must leave soon. There are a few more things you should know that will help you succeed in your journey.

"Once the soldiers that were sent by Lanier's father to disperse the stone had entered the cavern, I managed to call forth a great earthquake that caused great panic among our people and enemies alike. Fortunately, as I have previously related, because of this situation they only were able to remove one quarter of the stone. But that was enough, as the Stone was now incomplete, and the power of the Sun King to rule Chandi vanished. As it was not an easy task to move the wedge of stone, because it was heavy and cumbersome, they carted it away, up the trail of the cavern leading to the outside world using a cart pulled by strong men and horses.

"Once the infidels escaped the cavern, the piece of stone was lost, as Chandians cannot survive when leaving our world as it is now. Only a Chawa can leave the Kingdom and return. No other can do this. Not even I. And even then, the Chawa cannot take anything with him nor can he return with anything from the outer world. This is why the Stone was not reunited through our own efforts.

"When the Stone was diminished, the fate of our Kingdom fell into evil and unworthy hands. My only alternative to protect Chandi was to cast a spell on it. I created a new plane of time and dimension on which to preserve Chandi in order to neutralize the power of Lanier. This is why we have been at least able to survive without totally succumbing to her evil intentions. The spell can only be recanted with the reunification of the Stone, when the power of Chandi will be restored to overcome the evils of Lanier. Make no mistake, Shandru, that Chandi is real, but without a physical reality."

I thought of the Stone I had seen in the Lagoon, right before Chawa had disappeared and I was captured by the cannibals.

"The cannibals! Will I have to see them again?" I asked with dread.

"Yes, Shandru, as the Stone is in their sacred territory. You are destined to meet them again. Only this time, you will be prepared."

Mur crossed the room and stood in silence. His was solemn, calm. I was fearful, unsure still of my charge. Not very long after, Mur turned and faced me. It was as if he was reading my mind.

"Shandru, you saw the South stone on the lagoon. Chawa led you there."

"Yes, I saw it, " I replied. "It was very peaceful. No trouble seemed to lurk around it."

"Well, by now you know that isn't true. The stone has become something of a treasure to those savages and they guard it fiercely, though they haven't the slightest idea of its meaning or power. They often move it to different locations. Sometimes they place it in their sacred place in the jungle's heart. Other times they bring it back to the lagoon where you saw it. That valley is their hunting area. For many, many years, during the rainy season in the jungle, they migrated to this valley to hunt and live. Eventually, they drove many from the territory. We've learned much about them from the Chawas who have ventured forth over the years in search of you."

"How did the cannibals come to have this stone?" I asked.

"We only can surmise that Lanier's robbers, believing that they had escaped with the Stone from Chandi, stopped to rest or refresh the animals in the lagoon. Of course, they couldn't survive in the outer world and they must have been attacked or taken by surprise by these natives."

I quickly addressed my next concern. "Mur, if armed men are not capable of defending themselves against these natives, how can you expect me to go alone and fight against them; defeat them, and still recover your treasure?"

"Shandru, the ordination you participated in last evening was your initiation into the animal Kingdom. It brought you strength and power, supremacy over the rest of your fellow beings," he explained.

I looked at my "new" right arm, the glove with its sharp claws extending menacingly from the paw.

"Your new sandals are capable of taking you to places no ordinary person dare tread. They will help you leap great distances with no trouble at all. Your cape is impossible to destroy while you are wearing it. It is like a second skin—impenetrable. The pouch about your neck contains magic herbs. They cure every hurt or ailment common to man by chewing on only a few leaves. The glove is so powerful that, with a single stroke, you can rip apart anything that might attack you. Shandru, be assured that you are well-equipped to deal with any challenge. You now have heightened senses and the instinct to survive. You will have other abilities, that you will discover as you go. Remember to keep close to your heart this promise: that is, as the crane flies, so will you fly; as the kudu that runs like the wind, so shall you run; the elephant's strength will be yours, as will the monkey's cleverness. But above all, remember always the supremacy of the Leopards.

"But be on guard, Shandru, for the final challenge. Lanier will wait patiently. When she believes you have lowered your guard, she will strike. Beware of this evil creature and her deceptions!" warned Mur emphatically.

"The key to retaining her power is to keep the great Stone incomplete. As long as she does, we are powerless."

"And what shall protect me from her?"

Mur couldn't have been clearer. "Your instincts and your wits....and the crystal."

"The crystal?" I felt for it in my waist band. It was still there. "Of what use shall it be?" I asked.

"When the time comes, you will know and rely on it," Mur said.

"And if something happens to me, what exactly will happen to Elizabeth? What will become of her?"

"Your absence would result in Elizabeth's death."

"You'll kill her?" I started toward him.

Mur raised his hand, causing me to stop abruptly. "Of course not! We are peaceful people. But Lanier is powerful, indeed, and will enact her vengeance."

"But Mur, she is innocent," I protested.

"You seem not to understand, Shandru. Lanier has a heart empty of anything save jealousy and evil."

"Can't you protect her," I asked, "with some of your magic?"

"I'm afraid not, Shandru. That is the way it is."

"If that is the case, I must speak to Elizabeth at once and hear what she has to say about this. She must be warned of her predicament and what awaits her." I started towards the door.

"There is not enough time," Mur said. "For now, she is fine and will be better still when you return to take her back home again. Think positive."

"In that case, I see no need to put off what must be done. I shall leave immediately," I said, and waited for a response from Mur. There was none. He just extended his hand and took mine, squeezing it tightly. Again, he bowed low then led me from the room.

Our descent from the Kudus' Tower went unnoticed, or so I had hoped. We crossed the Hanging Bridge and made our way to the Temple of Courage.

As I stood in the temple, I let my gaze wander around the landscape.

Mur smiled, aware, I'm sure, of all my thoughts and misgivings.

"Are you ready?" he gently asked. I nodded. "Then may the good love of the Sun God protect you and help you on your way."

"Wait. Are there any guards in the Cavern? Or at the great falls?" I asked.

"Don't worry about them," Mur said. "They will be sleeping," he winked.

I turned and began making my way to the roaring waterfall, careful to stay in the shadows to avoid notice. I hesitated, and thought of returning to Elizabeth, in spite of Mur's command. But for some reason, my feet carried me unceasingly toward my destiny.

CHAPTER 32

THE REUNION

As I approached the waterfall, I saw no one, which was rather strange. There always seemed to be some sort of activity going on in the Kingdom. Except for the sound of the waterfall, I heard nothing; not a bird, nor the cry of some lonely animal.

Suddenly, to my right, a flock of birds flapped their way skyward, obviously disturbed by something. My newly-acquired acute hearing caught the cracking of a branch and the rustle of undergrowth. I immediately slowed my pace and prepared to defend myself. I stopped to hide behind a baobab tree, my gloved hand at the ready. I was sure that someone was there. "Who's there?" I roared. "Come out and show yourself."

There was more rustling in the vegetation and finally, a figure emerged. I was overcome with relief and joy.

"Elizabeth! My heavens, what are you doing here?" I asked, rushing to her side.

She recoiled briefly, frightened.

"Please. Don't be afraid. It's me, Alan." I tried to explain in a hurry. Then it struck me, I could again speak and communicate with her!

It was as if the floodgates of her emotions had been opened. "I know it's you, I realized it the other evening in my room, just after you left, but I'm so confused. What is that strange looking claw on your right hand? And what is that spotted cape? Where have you been? I've been asking for you for days! If it hadn't been for the old woman's reassurance, I might have given up hope of ever seeing you again."

Old woman? I asked myself. What old woman? My guard was up.

"Come here," I said, motioning her to my side. There was no hesitation, and she immediately joined me. She kept looking at me, wide-eyed.

"Alan, is there a logical explanation for all this? For the way you're dressed? For your deserting me?" she wanted to know.

"Elizabeth, there is much to tell you. But first, tell me why you're here?"

"I followed you. I managed to outwit the two guards at my door. The other evening, after you had visited me, I knew that I could escape by climbing down the vines that grew up the side of the palace to my balcony. Please don't be angry with me." She bit her lip.

"I just had to know why we were separated and why you were out of my sight for eight whole days, without contacting me or giving me any warning. Were you being held prisoner? In that Tower?"

"You knew I was in the Kudus' Tower?" I was surprised.

"Not until I saw you leave in that old priest's company. I was hiding in the bushes because I don't know who to trust. When I saw you, I began to follow you. I want to know what is happening!" she demanded. " I had a terrible time keeping up with you. In fact, at one point, only a few moments ago, I had lost sight of you and didn't know where you had gone or where you were headed. I was on the verge of giving up when I met the old woman, who said that she knew where you were headed, and pointed me in the right direction."

"What woman?"

"You mean you didn't see her? She's right over there." Elizabeth pointed over to the underbrush from where she had emerged. There was no one there. She looked around, confused.

If there was a woman, she was gone and that clearly disturbed Elizabeth. It also aroused my suspicions.

"Alan, how could she just vanished like that?" she asked.

"I haven't seen anyone, much less an old woman. But I don't doubt that you did. Was there anything unusual about her?" I asked. "Did she have blue eyes?" I had to be sure.

"Yes. Yes! So you did see her," Elizabeth exclaimed in relief.

I immediately pulled Elizabeth next to me, protecting her. I looked around, searching for Lanier.

"No. But I know who it was. She's a witch and she lives around here." I decided to keep my explanation ambiguous for now.

"How do you know that she is a witch?" Elizabeth questioned.

"It's a long story, but promise that you believe me. Tell me, is there anything else? Did she say anything or do anything? How did she help you?" I asked.

"She told me that you would be back soon, and I should just wait here with the monkeys until you returned. She was very kind. I was very thirsty, and she kindly shared her sweetened nectars with me. It was very refreshing and it tasted very good," she said.

"You drank what? How much?" I was afraid of her answer.

"Only a few swallows. The old woman said it would refresh me and would relieve my anxiety. She was right."

"Are you feeling all right?" I wanted to know.

"Well, why wouldn't I?" she asked.

I ignored her question, and I looked at her carefully. It was then that I noticed that she seemed to have lost weight. She also (probably my imagination) seemed younger. She changed the subject.

"Alan, you still haven't told me why are you dressed in this strange outfit." She looked me over, very curious about my attire.

I had been so happy to see her that I had momentarily forgotten completely about where I was headed. I suddenly realized that we had spent far too much time here, and we were very vulnerable. I would tell her everything that had happened to me later. But I had a decision to make right now. One that concerned Elizabeth.

Mur the magician had clearly told me that I would be on my own. Time was short. Should I take Elizabeth back to the Palace or should I take her with me to save time? I was convinced she had met up with Lanier, posing as the old woman. If I left her, Lanier might act to harm her. If I took her with me, she would be exposed to any danger lying ahead - like the cannibals. I had also learned that, with Elizabeth, trouble always seemed right around the corner. But I couldn't leave her here to fend for herself. It didn't require much rumination, so, after weighing all the possibilities (as far as I could realistically do), I decided to take her with me and take our chances together.

I took her hand. "Listen, Elizabeth. There is so much to tell you, but now is not the time. I will tell you about it as we go. Just trust me when I say that you and I are in much danger. We must leave this place NOW. We have already spent far too much time here. I don't know who is watching us, or what lies ahead. We have escaped danger together before. We can do it again."

With that, I turned and tugged on her arm. "Come. We've got to go through the falls."

SHANDRU & ELIZABETH

CHAPTER 33

THE RESCUE

The water was very cold and our leap through the falls completely soaked Elizabeth's clothing. The water had no effect on my leopard skin shroud and the water beaded up and dripped onto the ground. I looked up and saw the two orange flowers that had marked our exit from the falls only a few days before. The climb to the ledge above wasn't going to be easy. The rocks were wet and slippery and the path to the top was muddy. Even so, Elizabeth and I carefully made our way to the top, weaving in and out of the stones. I offered my hand when she faltered. She was quite out of breath when we finally reached the ledge, so we paused.

"Are you sure that you want to continue?" I asked. "It isn't going to get any easier. We have to be alert and prepared to meet what awaits us."

"I'll do fine. I won't be a hindrance. I promise." she replied.

I looked at her carefully. She appeared especially youthful today. Perhaps it was the way the wet clothes clung to her body. I took her hand and led her through the cave.

I slowed and proceeded cautiously as we came to the opening to the cavern. the glow was as before, warm and subtle, but illuminated the cavern in a fabulous array of gold, red and black shadows. The stone bridge was still intact, spanning the crevasse between this opening high above the cavern floor and the top of the monolith across the way. It was eerily quiet, and only the dripping of water resonated throughout the hollowness of the cavern.

I sensed an ominous quality to the atmosphere and it dawned on me that the cheerful chatter of the monkeys was absent. Elizabeth took my hand I implored her not to look down as we carefully inched our way across the bridge, as any misstep would see us plunging to the floor below. Finally, we arrived to the safety and solid ground of the monolith.

I immediately went to the altar. Just as I had remembered, the magnificent Sun Stone lay on top of the altar. The soft light of the cavern reflected off of it, causing very small shadows to be cast from the etchings. The quarter of stone that was missing, indeed, made it appear unfinished, incomplete. The vacant hole at the axis caused me to again touch my waistband to find the crystal. Its hard lump reassured me.

I looked at the empty space where the missing stone had rested for years, quite a large space. I tested one of the other stones by pushing on it. It was so heavy it resisted my efforts. I wondered as to how in heaven was I going to get the missing stone (if I was successful in retrieving it) from the cavern floor to the top of this monolith.

I looked around me. Surely there had to be a way. Lanier's thieves had taken it down, and if it were pushed over the edge, it would have smashed into a hundred pieces on the cavern floor. Looking over the edge of the monolith, I caught sight of four very sturdy ropes, made from some kind of fibers I had never seen before. Their ends were wrapped several times around the base of the altar. The other ends coiled on the cavern floor below. It was obvious to me that the stone had been carefully lowered from the monolith using these cords. I filed this away in my memory. Raising such a heavy stone back up to the top of this tall precipice was a different matter, one that I would confront if I should even find the stone again and could actually retrieve it and get it here. The enormity of this challenge almost overwhelmed me. I dismissed the thought and again took Elizabeth's hand.

"Come. We've little time." I said, as I started toward the spiral staircase that led to the floor of the cavern. I didn't mention it to Elizabeth, but my senses felt another presence—something cold and evil.

We carefully made our way across the seven white stones that poked their heads above the silent waters that separated the monolith from the sides of the cavern. From there, it was easy to find our way out. We hiked up the gentle grade of the trail that zigzagged up the side of the great cave, and found ourselves standing at the open stone door that had allowed access to the cavern. We passed through, stumbling occasionally, and worked our way to the cave entrance. I wondered if we would really come out again to our world.

Finally, we arrived at the mouth of the tunnel, where Elizabeth and I had spent our first night together, after our great escape from the natives and hyenas. Sure enough, I recognized the entrance as it was still partially blocked by the rock barrier we had made. I pushed the rocks aside and we emerged from the darkness to bright sunshine. From the position of the sun in the sky, I guessed that it was about 10 in the morning. We stopped and gazed out over the savannah below. With a sense of relief, a wave of familiarity swept over me. This wasn't really home, I thought to myself, but it was my world. The wildlife roamed below and the birds flew free and without care. It was hard to imagine any hardship that awaited me with the serenity that spread out before us.

We decided to rest briefly, which would allow Elizabeth's still-damp clothes to dry. Two enormous cranes soared above us, and their cries caught my attention. I watched them carefully, my intuition restless. It was then that I closed my eyes and found myself, in my mind, far above the earth, soaring and flying, as if I, too, were a crane. I could see for miles, and could see even the smallest creature below. I suddenly opened my eyes, and saw Elizabeth sitting quietly, shaking the last drops of water out of her hair. I closed my eyes again only to find myself seeing the world from the crane's perspective. Could it be that I could see the world through the creature's eyes if I wanted to? Was this one of my newly-acquired abilities? I was unsure, but the mere thought of that possibility was exciting, and it certainly might come in handy if it were true.

Suddenly, I became aware of the loud snorting of a pack of four kudus at the foot of the slope. Their incredible horns seemed perfectly sculptured. It might have been my imagination, but their gray coat seemed to glow unnaturally. Elizabeth dozed quietly next to me. Again, to my surprise, she seemed so young. Our time apart had apparently muddled my memory of her age. I had thought she was older, but she didn't look a day over eighteen.

I shook Elizabeth. "Wake up. We must get going," I said.

Elizabeth roused quickly and sat up. "Please, Alan," she said. "Please tell me what is going on. You were so vague earlier."

She was right about being informed. I briefly explained what had happened to me after her disappearance: the celebrations, Inzer, the delivery of the leopard twin, and finally, about my encounters with Mur and the Sun King. I told her about the prophecies and my commission, as the Shandru, to reunite the Sun Stone and assume leadership of Chandi as King. Surprisingly, my tale was completely accepted. Satisfied, Elizabeth simply nodded her understanding. Again I was struck by what a brave woman she was…or did I mean brave girl?

With renewed spirit, I disclosed my plan to her.

We made our way down the slope and headed toward the place where I had seen the wedge of the missing Sun Stone piece days earlier. The kudus followed us for some reason. They kept up, and paused only occasionally to eat.

Elizabeth, not acting her usual self, seemed particularly rebellious, behaving as a teenager would. After only an hour of hiking, she suddenly became cranky and would stop every four or five steps, whining and complaining. The cranes that had accompanied us had now flown away, impatient with my slowing progress. Amazingly, one of the kudus approached and nudged me. I took advantage of this friendly posture and picked Elizabeth up and sat her on his back. Our progress hastened after that. Soon, we reached a clearing, through which ran a refreshing stream. It was here that the two cranes were waiting for us. I helped Elizabeth off and she quickly went to the stream and drank. The kudus grazed nearby.

I sat under a tree, lowered my head and concentrated, willing one of the cranes to fly. Once in the air, through his eyes, I saw Elizabeth and myself below by the stream, lost among the fallen trees and thickets. From that view, I saw what looked like two cannibals approaching us. I followed their progress from the air. It wouldn't be long before they came upon us. Back to earth, I hissed to Elizabeth and signaled for her to be quiet. She sensed danger and quietly made her way to my side.

The distance between the cannibals and us diminished, for I easily detected their scent. Mur had been right about my acute senses.

It was time to test out my other acquired powers. Apparently, I could transform myself into a leopard just by willing it. And certainly there was no better time for me to do that. I closed my eyes and began to exert my will over my body. I felt a change surge through me. I looked over at Elizabeth. She was paralyzed with fear. She didn't move a muscle. I turned and followed my nose in the direction of the approaching cannibals.

I stealthily moved through the bush as a leopard, aware of my strength, anxious for a kill. With a roar I propelled myself upon the two, who were terrified at the mere sight of me as a leopard man. My claw slashed out quickly and deadly. They tried to defend themselves, but to no avail. I simply overpowered them. It took only seconds. Suddenly, I was myself again. Feeling a strange satisfaction that both repulsed and pleased me, I dipped my bloodied claw/hand into the nearby stream. My thoughts turned toward Elizabeth.

I found my way back along the stream, only to find her gone. I surveyed the area, looking for her. I sniffed with my new senses, and found her scent wafting through the air. I quietly began to track her scent. I heard rustling ahead of me, and muffled cries for help. I peered through the thick foliage to see Elizabeth being led away by the natives. She had been captured again!

I was blinded by anger. Flush with new-found confidence, my immediate reaction was to pounce on these savages. I controlled my impulses, thinking of the harm they might do to Elizabeth. I followed the natives until they disappeared into their village.

I circled the village, staying in the shadows and dark cover of the jungle. Now dark, a bonfire provided the only light. From the cover of night, I looked around and saw many of the savages' faces from my previous incarceration. Though I scanned the scene carefully, I couldn't locate Elizabeth. My concern heightened.

I crept to the other side of the village where the largest gathering of natives were congregated.

The savages' dark skin glistened with sweat and their painted faces portrayed evil. They were focused on what was before them. The big fat fellow, the one who had belittled and ridiculed me what seemed like a lifetime ago, held a long tree branch with a bloody piece of meat on one end. It wasn't human, because a zebra carcass lay nearby. He waved the meat over a muddy pond, trying to lure a huge crocodile out of the murky water. Before long, the incredibly large crocodile shot from the water, straight up, and locked its jaws around the bloody morsel, which quickly disappeared through its razor-sharp teeth.

I retreated to the surrounding darkness. I needed to find Elizabeth—immediately. I searched the skies for my crane friends, and though I concentrated as hard as I could, I couldn't locate them. Sensing trouble was close, I climbed a tree for refuge. Although my view was obstructed by trees and branches, I was still aware of the twenty or thirty natives just a few feet away. I evaluated the situation. Sooner or later, I thought, the natives would have to sleep.

Resting my eyes, I saw a troubling vision. I saw the wedge of the missing piece of Sun Stone resting in the middle of the lagoon and a young girl, no more than twelve years old, bound to the stone with a wrapping of vines and ropes. Struggling to free herself, her eyes were filled with desperation.

I sat up with a jolt. I rubbed my eyes, trying to erase this vision from my mind. My thoughts were interrupted by the sound of drums. Their pounding originated from somewhere deep in the jungle, not from the village—the village was empty.

I willed myself to relax and closed my eyes again, hoping for guidance.

I jumped from my perch. Led by scent and the sound of drumbeats, I bounded to the source. The jungle was dense, but the drums became louder, and the stench of the savages grew stronger.

I came to a familiar lagoon. There, in the middle of its calm waters, was the wedge of Sun Stone. But distress quickly overcame any feeling of excitement when

I saw that, true to my dream, a very young girl, dressed in a white gown, was tied securely to its face. I carefully crept through the tight foliage, towards the edge of the lagoon.

Then, leaping from nowhere, Samo the small monkey, landed on my shoulder and pulled on my ear, almost pulling it from my head. He was jumping and crying, seeming to prevent my approaching the lagoon.

When he had my complete attention, he jumped to the nearest tree. He reached up and plucked a huge, heavy seed from the branch in front of him. He threw it to the jungle's floor, where it was swallowed up immediately.

Quicksand! I looked up at Samo the monkey to offer my thanks, but he was gone.

I avoided the deadly trap and made my way to the edge of the lagoon. The wedge of stone stood alone, standing proudly in the glorious sun. The young girl slumped severely, held into a standing position by the tightly wound ropes. She appeared unconscious. Perhaps she had been drugged.

I stopped myself from calling out. I sensed the savages still about, but where? I had to get the attention of the girl, to let her know I was there to help. I picked up a small rock and tossed it toward her. It plunked loudly in the water. She swayed her head groggily, but didn't awaken. I tried again. This time, the rock landed close enough to splash her, causing her to arouse.

She looked around, then her eyes locked on mine.

"Alan," she cried. "Please help me!"

"Elizabeth?" I couldn't believe it. Surely this wasn't Elizabeth. This was only a child! Then I thought of the nectar that the old woman, Lanier, had offered to Elizabeth just before she found me in Chandi. It was apparent that Lanier used her evil magic to cast a spell on Elizabeth, causing her to regress in age.

I ignored the threat of the savages attacking me and waded into the lagoon toward Elizabeth and the Stone. To my dismay, I found it was protected by crocodiles, dozens of them. Obviously, the cannibals felt these were guardians enough.

I had to act fast. First, I had to distract the crocodiles.

Thankfully, my leopard senses alerted me. I smelled the sentry before I saw him. He was standing against a tree, his back to me. He was oblivious to my presence, dancing in position to the beat of the drums that had begun only moments before. I approached, stealthily. When I got to within a meter or so, I stepped on a dry branch. The loud cracking alerted the sentry. He turned, spear in hand. But when he saw me, his eyes widened and his body stiffened in fright. Before he could utter any warning, or a prayer, I lashed out at him with my clawed glove, ripping his body from throat to waist. Blood squirted from his neck as his body hit the ground. Mercifully, death came quickly.

I was running out of time. I dug into the carcass and excised a large piece of flesh. I threw it into the water. It landed a few meters in, splashing loudly. The crocodiles immediately recognized the smell of food. They splashed violently, each trying to be the first to get the meat. I pulled another chunk from the carcass, again throwing it toward the lagoon. This time, the morsel didn't make it to the water, but certainly attracted the crocs. I continued to do this until a trail of meat led to the dead cannibal. The crocodiles fought over each piece, but my purpose was accomplished. There were no longer any crocs in the lagoon.

In the clearing where Chawa and I had originally set up camp, the four kudus, who had followed Elizabeth and I from the cave, were quietly eating some leaves. They had, for some reason, continued to follow me wherever I went. I quietly waded back out of the water and approached the kudu. All four had those beautiful blue, sapphire eyes. With their help, I improvised a device to transport the Stone. With my sharp claws, I managed to separate some very strong branches from a tall ironwood tree and fashioned a cart, albeit one without wheels. I bound the branches together with the available vines that weaved throughout the jungle, and made a solid frame. Using smaller branches, I criss-crossed them over the frame, creating a surface on which the Stone could be laid. I found some more vines and made a crude yoke to place around the four kudus' necks. I yoked the kudus, and, while lifting the transport, backed them into the lagoon and toward the Stone and Elizabeth.

When I freed her from her bonds, she jumped into my arms and hugged me desperately.

She sobbed, "I don't understand what is happening, Alan. Why am I in a ten year-old body?"

I carried her to the lead kudu and set her on top of it, trying to come up with an answer. "The only reason I can think of is that this has something to do with the drink the old woman gave you back in Chandi. I believe she was Lanier, who has every intention of preventing your return to Chandi. We must, somehow, get back to Mur. He must have an antidote to stop this regression. I don't want you disappearing before my eyes."

Although it wasn't easy, things happened as I planned. The four kudus, yoked together, backed up, paying little attention to the water that now reached their shoulders. The transport now was firmly up against the base that held the Stone erect. I went behind the Stone, and began to push, rocking the Stone back and forth. After a few moments, the Stone toppled from its moorings and splashed heavily into the pool. Thankfully, it landed squarely in the middle of the transport, face down. I whooped a cry of victory. My victory shout startled the kudus, who launched into a frenzied run, pulling the stone from the lagoon. They disappeared into the jungle. I chased after them, amazed to find a leopard was leading them.

We traveled briskly for a few hours and then stopped to rest. Even with their magical strength, the kudus had become tired with their heavy burden. I freed them from their yoke. They drank from a nearby stream. When they returned, they lowered their majestic head so I could again attach them to their precious load. It was time to continue.

Again, I put Elizabeth on the back of the lead kudu. Suddenly, the air was filled with flying lances and spears. The savages had found us and were determined to finish the job the crocodiles had failed to do.

The kudus broke into a run, carrying away a tearful Elizabeth and the heavy, sacred stone. Elizabeth and the Stone disappeared down the path. I turned to find the savages were more interested in me than in them. I was completely surrounded by angry cannibals, spears pointed right at me.

The fat chief emerged from the ring of savages. Furiously, he barked some orders and all action stopped. He seemed to be at odds with a tall, young fellow who was outrageously painted from head to toe. Shaking his spear at the chief, he seemed to get the better of the argument. With lance in hand, he waved off the chief and started towards me. With that, the rest rushed at me and shoved their lance tips into every available spot on my body. With little to lose, I opened my mouth and bellowed a leopard roar. Not even a moment passed when my roar was joined by others. The natives stopped, frozen in surprise. They saw that they were surrounded by twelve huge, ferocious leopards, who walked back and forth, pacing menacingly, coughing roars from hell.

The natives now became the prey. They backed away from me in panic. Some scattered into the jungle. I grabbed the fat chief and introduced him to my clawed glove. His skin opened like a rotten gourd and he fell to the ground without a sound.

All around me there was screaming and crying. As blood splattered all around, one by one, the cannibals met their end. It was not a fair battle and it didn't last long. I looked for the tall savage who had been about to plunge his spear into me. He had somehow escaped the leopards' attack and caught me off-guard as I scanned the

SHANDRU & THE CANNIBALS

bloody chaos. He grabbed me from behind by my throat, choking off my windpipe. I twisted and managed to claw his legs viciously. His grip lessened in his pain. but he was surprisingly strong. We grappled furiously, and I couldn't get the upper hand. I sensed another savage, turned my head and saw a wicked smile as the savage poised his spear for a deadly plunge. I gathered all my strength, still in the iron clutch of my foe, and wrenched around, so that the spear meant for me plunged into his back. The savage loosened his hold on me, as the life left his eyes. He fell to the ground. Without any hesitation, I challenged the last one, roaring violently. After the shortest pause, he turned and ran into the jungle, hoping to escape. A bad choice. I heard a blood-curdling roar and a few horrible cries, then silence. My leopard brothers had the last word.

I left the carnage and ran swiftly in the direction the kudus had raced, hoping to overtake them. Racing down the trail, I feared for Elizabeth's condition. How was I going to accomplish my mission and save Elizabeth at the same time?

LANIER

Darkness was overtaking the day as I reached the slope. I had followed the kudus' trail, which was clearly marked by sixteen sunken hoof marks, a testimony to the heavy cargo they bore.

Questions and concerns bombarded my mind. What was I going to do with Elizabeth? What about Lanier? Should I return to Mur the Magician? How much time did I really have? And, even more troubling, I knew that once I got back to the cavern with the Stone, I still had to get it up the monolith and join it with the other three stones.

I climbed the slope to the cave's entrance. There, much to my relief, I was met by an anxious welcoming committee. The cranes were noisy and clearly disturbed by the four nervous kudus, who were still tied together and yoked to the transport. Elizabeth, who now looked to be about six years old, was fast asleep, lying on one of the kudus backs. I was thankful for her escape, though painfully aware of the spell Lanier had cast over her. My inability to do anything about it tortured me. What had she done to deserve such an evil ordeal?

I unfastened her from the kudu and tenderly placed her over my shoulder. I headed into the cave and the kudus obediently followed me, bearing their precious cargo. It was slow going, with rock croppings impeding progress at times. But the kudus managed to squeeze through the meandering passageways and pull the stone behind them.

I felt a bit of relief as we finally came upon the ledge that overlooked the cavern. The deep glow had not changed, but there seemed to be much more of a chill in the air. Again, I felt an evil presence. The kudus followed me down the path to the edge of the moat surrounding the looming monolith.

I crossed the moat, stepping carefully on each of the seven stones that connected to the island where the monolith stood. I lay Elizabeth, still sleeping, against one of its smooth walls and returned to the water's edge. I beckoned the kudus to forge the moat. Without hesitation, slowly and carefully, the kudus waded into the water, dragging the Stone behind them. Suddenly, the kudus, the transport and the Stone

LANIER, SHANDRU & YOUNG ELIZABETH

disappeared under the water's surface and my heart stopped.

Then, behind me, a familiar voice broke the silence.

"Tani?" I blurted. I turned smiling. Inzer must have sent her to help me, I thought.

"You've come so far, only to lose the Stone to the moat," the voice said.

My jaw dropped when I saw it wasn't Tani. This person was beautiful, except for those ice-cold blue eyes. They were lifeless, perhaps the result of too much evil and not enough happiness in her life. Like Mur, Lanier appeared ageless. But unlike Mur, she exuded evil, and what she had done to Elizabeth was unacceptable.

Her raspy, evil voice broke in. "Go back to where you came from. You can still do it and come to no harm. You have no interest here."

"And if I refuse?" I snorted.

She bravely walked toward me. Her thin lips showed a hint of a smile, alerting me that I would be no match for her powers. Instinctively, I returned my comical smile. She laughed!

"You're entertaining" she scoffed. "Like her..." She pointed towards the sleeping Elizabeth.

My anger continued to rise, unabated. "What do you want?" I screamed.

"You are starting to bore me. Don't you know that I can read your mind, know your deepest thoughts? You hate me, yet you find me beautiful. Isn't that what you are thinking?" Lanier demanded.

Witch! I thought to myself.

Lanier laughed. "Not a witch, Shandru. I am Lanier, a sorceress having more powers than you'll ever know!" she proudly proclaimed.

"What have you done to Elizabeth? What has she done to deserve this?" I demanded.

"Come now, Shandru, you know very well that she is the true queen of Chandi. But I will promise you that she will never take the throne. My throne."

I started towards her when the kudus emerged from the moat. They paused at the edge of the moat and allowed the water to slide off of their back. Then, with one final effort, they lunged forward and the Stone emerged, still tied to the rickety transport.

I turned to Lanier and smiled. "Not that powerful, Lanier?" I asked mockingly. I turned to go to Elizabeth.

Furious, Lanier blocked my way. "She's nothing more than a child," she argued.

"Her time is running out, as you can see. She is not long for this life. You must choose between her and your own life," she taunted.

Not bothering to answer, I shrugged and went around Lanier to Elizabeth and picked her up. Holding her close to my chest, I didn't move, unsure of Lanier's reaction. Lanier smiled, obviously savoring my discomfort. She then turned and went to the edge of the moat. Curiously drawn to her, I followed. As I reached the water's edge, it began to churn. I stepped back, astounded as a giant bubble rose from its depths and rolled across its surface to Lanier. To my utter amazement, she stepped inside the bubble and motioned me to join her. Against my conscious judgment (perhaps she had cast a spell on me), I entered. My equilibrium was shaken, and I tried to steady myself, leaning a hand against one of its walls. Much to my amazement, my hand went right through the bubble. Surely we would start going under, drowning in all this surrounding water.

"Relax. Bring your hand inside. We are going down. Don't worry. My magic is most powerful," Lanier spoke smugly with confidence.

High above Lanier's head, the biggest python head opened its mouth and its tongue slithered in and out.

My right hand now rested over Elizabeth, who continued sleeping.

"Where are you taking us?" I asked.

The water was extremely murky. I saw water, heard water, felt water and knew water was all around, yet I didn't feel wet. My own sweat was the only real moisture I was aware of, and it ran freely down my back. Soon the bubble came to a stop. Lanier stepped outside and offered me her hand.

"Welcome to my home," she beckoned.

"Home?" I looked around. I was surrounded by enormous walls of fire. They burned hot and endlessly, but I seemed immune to their heat. The floor was like a swirling liquid. I could walk on it, yet not sink. It felt more solid than it appeared.

Lanier walked to a throne and sat down haughtily. Her throne was comprised of seven python snakes, carefully entwined to form a seat. Their tails formed the throne's legs and the impressive heads were living decorations of the backrest. High above Lanier's head, the biggest python head opened its mouth and its tongue slithered in and out.

I turned to look at the room. It was a huge and had a monumental window opening out to the Valley of Chandi. I tried to cross to the window, only to crash into something solid but invisible, awakening Elizabeth. I put my hands against this invisible wall. It felt cold, smooth, impenetrable. No finger, hand or fist could pass through it.

"This open window to the valley, is it real?" I asked.

"As real as a crystal ball, or a vessel full of water, or a pool of blood. What if I told you that, in order to escape from me now, you shall have to walk through a living hell? It is not impossible to survive, but I guess it would be quite a challenge, even for someone like you. Are you frightened of heights? How do you feel about things that crawl? Perhaps you would like to know the easy way out of this place? I can and will help you out—in exchange for one or two little favors. I'm very easy to please." Lanier tried to tempt me.

"Pleasing any woman is a hard thing. I quit trying a long time ago," I quipped.

"You will be well on your way to satisfying me if you would forget about that young, blonde hindrance you're carrying. Let her disappear. Let her continue her regression into nothingness. Her voice overflowed with evil.

I scoffed at her request to dispose of Elizabeth and laughed in her face. It was then I learned, the hard way, that one shouldn't antagonize a witch. Before I knew it, everything around me went black.

I was rudely awakened by the icy water. Now fully conscious and aware of what was happening, I tried desperately to keep us both from sinking to our doom. I swam with all my strength. Survival was my focus as I fought the terrible currents. I became weary and where the waters calmed momentarily, I tried to rest by floating face up, with Elizabeth on my chest, wailing. It was a miracle she hadn't already drowned.

After what seemed like hours, the river heaved and threw us out, disgorging us on some rocky banks. Barely alive, I pulled the now-quiet infant next to me, and tried to determine if she was breathing. Amazingly, she was sound asleep. Relieved, I, too, fell into unconsciousness.

I was awakened by familiar sounds filling my ears. The sound of loud squawking became louder and louder, and I raised my head and looked to the sky. Cranes! They had come back.

I picked up Elizabeth, and, using the straps of my herb pouch, fastened her close to my chest. Revived, I tried to call out. I waved vigorously, hoping to attract the cranes' attention. They circled above me briefly, the swooped down, landing close by. Their mysterious green eyes glowed intelligently. One of them allowed me to mount his feathered back.

Once we were all airborne, I looked down to find that the river was not that wide.

We flew for some time. Below me the world spread out in all of its grandeur: greens, yellows and browns.

Before I could figure where we were going, the cranes quickly descended into a hole opening darkly into the earth below. We continued in darkness until, suddenly, the cranes swooped into a dimly lit, yet familiar area. The Cavern.

Circling and slowly descending, the cranes gently deposited Elizabeth and me at the base of the monolith. The Sun Stone glinted only a few meters away and, miraculously, were the stalwart kudus.

Having little time to ponder our escape from certain death and the evil Lanier, I found the ends of the fibrous vines that spilled from the top of the great monolith. I wrapped them around the Sun Stone and tied them securely to each other, forming a basket in which the Stone could rest.

Elizabeth began to cry. I looked over at her. She was little more than an infant. In desperation, I realized how little time was left to save her. I rushed to the spiral staircase and climbed to the top of the temple. I found the other ends of the vines and wrapped them around the base of the altar, hoping to use the base as a foothold, to pull the Stone up the side. I got in place and wrapped the vines around my arms and hands and began to pull. I pulled with all my might. The Stone didn't budge. Not even a centimeter. I tried again, pulling with all my "magical" strength. My muscles strained, but to no avail.

Quickly, I went to the edge of the monolith and looked down. Nothing there except Elizabeth, the cranes, the stone and the four kudus. The kudus, of course, were the key to my plan. Moving rapidly, I went back to the altar and untied the ends of the vines. I tested their strength. Satisfied, I tied the ends of the vines together, creating one long rope, making sure that the vines wrapped securely around the base of the altar. I tossed the loose end over the edge, where it landed a small distance from the stone. I bounded down the spiral stairs three steps at a time.

I reached the bottom and went to the Stone, working as fast as I could. I created a new bond between stone and vine by wrapping the vine around the stone until it was secure. I then called the kudus to me. With the free end of the vine, I wove it in and out of the yoke still on their neck and tested the knot. It was as good as it was going to get.

I shouted at the kudus, and slapped each on their hindquarters. They moved away from the monolith and the vine tightened, first up the monolith and then down the other side. I yelled again. The kudus continued their steady movement and the stone began to slide to the monolith's base. I slapped them again and they lunged forward, pulling the stone upright, where it dangled a millimeter above the ground.

"Yoooweeeeeaaaahhh," I shouted. Slowly, the wedge of jade ascended the side of the monolith. The kudus reach the moat's edge but continued on, entering the water, going deeper and deeper, but they didn't stop and the Stone continued to rise. I raced up the stairs again and reached the top just as the Stone eased over the side. The kudus to continued to pull and the Stone slid toward the altar.

I realized if the kudus continued, they would pull the stone around the altar and, eventually, over the side of the monolith again, this time causing the Stone to crash to the floor below, on top of baby Elizabeth! I ran to the edge of the monolith and found the kudus had emerged to the other side of the moat. I shouted at them to halt and amazingly, they stopped. I whistled once and they backed off briefly, allowing me to readjust the vine so it went over the top of the altar, hopefully allowing the kudus to then pull the Stone into place. I hesitated and looked over at baby Elizabeth. I realized I must gamble. To save Elizabeth, I had to outwit Lanier. I must get her to rescind her spell over Elizabeth before the Sun Stone is reunited, for that is when she loses her powers. If that happens before the spell is reversed, Elizabeth will be lost to me forever. I descended the stairs and mustered all my powers.

"Lanier! Lanier!" I called out. "Wherever you are, come into the light where I can see you!"

Silence engulfed the cavern.

"Lanier,"I called again. "You win. I can please you. Please, just let Elizabeth live."

Silence.

"Anything. Anything you want!" I urged, using my most convincing voice.

Then, a strange, pulsating sensation began to vibrate all around. The air became heavy. Elizabeth felt it, too, and began to have trouble with her breathing. Panting myself, I stood up, only to find my knees could no longer support me. I felt as if I was suffocating. I picked up the gasping baby. I was losing her.

A wicked laughter echoed throughout the cavern.

"That is so much better. I am happy that you have seen it my way." Lanier said. She appeared from behind the great monolith. She swaggered cockily around us, pleased with the outcome. "You did say <u>anything</u>, didn't you?"

"Yes!" I tried to answer, barely able to breathe.

"Well, well. Elizabeth has ended up serving me very well,"she said slyly.

Air—fresh air—began to saturate the cavern. I tried to get up, only to find I hadn't yet recovered my strength entirely. Elizabeth's color returned to her face as she started breathing comfortably once more.

"Listen to me! Did you really think you can outwit me; fool me into reversing my spell on Elizabeth? My powers enable me to read your mind, you would-be Shandru," she laughed, mocking me.

"But the stone is not reunified. The final stone sits atop this monolith, still separated from the others. You have come so far, only to fail in the face of my power," she sneered. A menacing grin spread across her face.

Then, to my horror, I saw Lanier straighten up, turn sharply, and head towards Elizabeth. She picked her up and began to climb the spiral staircase. Her long dress swished as she went up the monolith. I followed desperately, planning my next move as I went.

When I reached the top of the stairs, I found Lanier standing before the stone altar, contemplating the three Stones, then placing the infant on the altar. The Stones had started to vibrate and a flashing bright light started to cover the altar, spreading across its surface, splashing on the floor and then across the wall of the cavern. Colors! All kinds of beautiful colors flashed around us, increasing in intensity with every passing moment. Reaching a crescendo, the dancing colors spun into a whirlpool of flashing lights that encircled us. My head began to spin, causing me to close my eyes and dizzily collapse on the ground.

CHAPTER 35

THE CONFRONTATION

I managed to stand and refocus. Lanier had removed a scepter from her gown and was babbling incoherently in front of the altar. The fury around her swirled to crescendo as she raised the glistening knife above her head. Elizabeth was crying ever more weakly.

"You dare to challenge me?"

"Lanier!" I shouted. "You're finished!" I pulled the glowing, green crystal from my waistband. As I waved it around, it shot a flurry of colors zigzagging across the roof of the cavern. The wind groaned even louder.

Her cold, dead, blue eyes locked on me. She slowly turned away from Elizabeth and hissed at me. "You dare to challenge me?" A bloodcurdling cry ripped over the din of the wind.

Right before me, to my extreme bewilderment, Lanier began to transform right before my eyes! She turned green, and her skin became scaly. Doubling in size in the blink of an eye, Lanier grew quite a snout, from which slime and vapors oozed. Again, she grew and a tail began to emerge. Running quickly to the altar, I grabbed Elizabeth and held her close. Still, Lanier grew and grew. I rushed to the stairs and placed Elizabeth three steps down, out of harm's way. Clutching my crystal, I returned to the top of the monolith where a completely transformed Lanier stood before me, roaring and breathing fire.

"You dare to challenge me?" boomed throughout the cavern. The voice was no longer human. A frightful, demon-possessed dragon stood before me.

I glanced at the altar, knowing it provided some modicum of protection. I ran towards it, but Lanier swung her deadly tail in my direction. It hit my right leg and I tripped, banging heavily into the altar. I peered over the edge, and saw that Lanier was coming around from the right. Like a shot, I darted to the left, only to be met head-on by Lanier, who had easily hopped over the altar into my path. No sooner had I regretted my move, she slapped me and I stumbled to the edge of the monolith. I dropped the lance that held the crystal and it bounced over the edge and clinked on the cavern floor below. I grasped furiously at the vine that draped over the side. It was the only thing to prevent my plunging to my death, but I missed, and started to fall.

I had fallen about thirteen meters, when I managed to grab hold of the vine. When I latched onto it, I stopped so abruptly I thought my arms would come out of their sockets. Yet I hung there, in agony.

That chilling laugh again filled the chamber, and I looked up. Lanier appeared, hoping to see how crumpled my body had become when it hit the cavern floor.

Just then, the kudus began to pull on the vine. With the tiniest movement, I felt myself being lowered. But too slowly. Lanier stood at the top, laughing, savoring the moment.

When I was about twenty six meters above the cavern floor. I heard a scream above me. Lanier's foot had become entangled in the vine, and she fell towards me. I winced and prepared for the impact, and the certain death that waited below me. But her fall abruptly stopped as the vine became taut, just as it had happened to me before. Bound by the same vine, we began to descend rapidly.

The added weight of the dragon caused the wedge of Sun Stone on top of the monolith to be pulled towards the altar, approaching unification. Above me, Lanier struggled to free herself. She did so and, as dragons do, sprouted her wings and flew right at me. I hung desperately to the rope. At the last possible moment, I used my legs and pushed away from the side of the monolith, swinging out away from it. Lanier roared as she flew by, missing me by a hair.

The kudus worked hard. They pulled and pulled the wedge of stone, ever so slowly! It was now only a meter away.

Lanier, perched on a ledge high above the monolith, regrouped. I was now about ten meters above the floor of the cavern and Lanier quickly diminished the gap between us. She took a deep breath and fire shot out of her mouth. I was going to meet my end in ashes.

I let go of the vine just as the searing heat reached me, and landed heavily on my feet. Lanier soared around the cave and slowly landed before me, ready for the kill.

"You dared to challenge me? The all-powerful Lanier?" she bellowed. Again, her laugh reverberated throughout the cavern. ***"Prepare to meet your end, Shandru."***

She took a deep breath, ready to sear me into nothingness, then suddenly stopped as the final wedge of Sun Stone kissed its long lost mates and locked into place. A confused look flooded Lanier's dragon face and I saw my chance with her pause. I rolled to the base of the great monolith and picked up my lance. It felt good in my hand and it glowed warmly.

I charged Lanier, catching her by surprise. She turned out of the way, but moved slower than before. The fire from her nose and mouth sputtered and soon was nothing but steam. Still, she was full of vitriol, and snarled at me menacingly. She swung her tail at me again, and, this time, I was able to leap over it and run full force at Lanier's soft underbelly. I let out a most ferocious leopard roar and plunged the crystal deep into her heart, twisted it a few times, and pulled it out, coated with a thick, red blood.

Lanier let out no scream, no laugh. She just froze. From the location of her gory wound began a cracking sound, as breaking glass. I couldn't believe my eyes – Lanier was actually crystallizing throughout her body. Crystal in hand, I backed away in astonishment. I looked up to see the final few centimeters of Lanier harden into a crystallized dragon.

Then everything went black and I lost consciousness.

"Alan!" Someone shook me. "Alan!" the voice sounded again. A familiar voice.

I slowly came around. I shook the cobwebs from my eyes. I felt as if I had been sleeping for days.

"Alan, are you all right?" I felt a soft hand against my cheek.

I looked up to find a worried Elizabeth stroking my face. A fully grown Elizabeth! The excitement was overwhelming and I reached out and pulled her close to me, hugging her all my strength.

"Oh, Elizabeth, I thought I would never see you again."

THE DRAGON LANIER

"You did it, Alan! You reunited the Stone," She said excitedly.

"What are you talking about?" I was still groggy.

"The Sun Stone. The kudus pulled it together. I saw it when I woke up. For some strange reason, I had been sleeping on the steps to the altar."

"The Sun Stone reunited?" I asked. I tried to remember. It was then I looked behind me. Looming large over me was the most interesting, ice-blue crystal dragon. Frozen for eternity. It was a perfect sculpture, except for the odd look on its face.

My heart skipped a beat when I realized that I had finished my quest. I got up and began to pace, hoping to release some of the pent-up energy. I was so excited. I looked at Elizabeth. My heart skipped another beat. I took her hand and we ascended the spiral staircase to the top of the monolith and across the narrow stone bridge to proclaim our victory to Chandi.

EPILOG

Our return to Chandi was cause for great celebration throughout the land. Word went far and wide: Shandru had restored power to Chandi by reuniting the Sun Stone. He has returned to the Palace to take his rightful place as the new Sun King, with the blue-eyed Elizabeth as queen. Or so the news went.

Mur was waiting for us as we entered the Temple. It was brightly lit, quite the opposite of my first visit here with him. Mur bowed low. "Welcome home, Honorable One, Shandru, Fulfiller of Prophecy. We shall be forever in your service."

I felt a deep, frightening emotion raising its ugly head, so much it prevented me from responding. I had my back to Mur. I kept silent.

Mur continued, "You must always remember: all men posses a powerful force, hidden within their soul, far more superior that any mortal can ever imagine. When it is awakened and brought into action, everything is possible and you will succeed."

"I will remember. Thank you for the advice," I answered. I handed him the glove, the cape, the sandals and the pouch. Mur carefully deposited them into a crystal urn and closed it. I changed into my old clothes; nobody told me to do it—it just felt right.I decided to be brief and to the point. "Mur, I have been honored to be able to serve the good people of Chandi and to bring to them a renewed hope and future. But I am not a King. I am a human being, from another world, another time.

"I'm tired and I want to go home," I finished.

"This is your birthplace! This <u>is</u> home for you!" Mur reproached me as he looked at Elizabeth, now the only blue-eyed beauty in this land. "And you, fair queen?"

Elizabeth came to my side and grasped my arm. "I am leaving with him. I, too, am tired. I want to go home...and be with the Shan.....er, Alan."

"It was written that this would come to pass," said Mur, who opened the box in the middle of the table and removed a golden scroll.

"What's that?" I asked. "I don't remember seeing that scroll."

Mur removed the golden twine that kept the parchment tightly rolled. He looked at me and then Elizabeth, and with a heavy sigh, read:

In the end, the Shandru,
Having re-established goodness and
Prosperity to you, glorious Chandi,
Shall take his leave from the land.
He shall hold his queen to his side
And count four sisters as his attendants,
No other shall depart.
The holy one of Chandi shall
Do his duty, and forever seal
Its doors, separating it from
The mortal world until such time
The Sun King's progeny shall rebuild
The Lost City in the outer world—
A magnificent tribute to the Shandru.

Mur stopped and rolled up the scroll. Silence filled the temple.

"I don't understand, Mur. What is that supposed to mean?" I asked.

"It has been foretold that you will return to your land. You, Elizabeth and your four sisters, the princesses of Chandi. You shall not return here again."

"Aw, sure I'll be back. What? You think I'd forget you…Sun King…Chandi? Of course I'll be back!" I admonished.

"No!" said Mur sadly, "You are to leave immediately. I have briefed your sisters and they are waiting for you. I have already recited the incantation to begin the process." With those words, the sun disappeared behind some quickly gathering thunderheads. The ground beneath me trembled.

"Before too long, Chandi will be sealed forever from your world. It will be so to protect our Sun Stone from those from your world that would wish us ill. It must be so, as the prophets have demanded it." Mur became unstable as the ground shook even more.

Over the past days, I had learned Mur was always serious. I could not ignore what he said, or question his conjectures. I didn't hesitate. I took Elizabeth's hand.

"Quickly. Back to the waterfall." I turned and pulled her to the Temple entrance.

As we ran out, we were met by my four sisters. They were laughing, and squealed brightly when they saw us, but their mood changed when the ground under their feet started to tremble again.

"Retronia. Tary. Hurry. Follow me!" I said it as sharply as I could, demanding action. "You, too, Lutrania and Kuiosa. There is little time."

We ran pass the sacred gong and headed toward the roaring waterfall. The rumbling of the earth increased with every step we took. My sisters screamed but kept pace. Elizabeth stayed right with me. All around us trees whipped and cracked.

Without even so much as a pause, we all jumped through the waterfall to the wet ground on the other side. No time to catch our breath. In the distance, the volcano began to smoke and send magma high into the air. I couldn't believe my eyes as I turned one last time back only to see my friend Samo running towards us. I opened my arms, and he jumped into them. Together once again, we all made our escape.

I reached the ledge of the tunnel first and helped Elizabeth and my sisters the final few steps. Assured they had made it unscathed, I led them into the tunnel to the rock bridge that spanned the cavern wall to the monolith.

"Hurry," I shouted. The shaking increased, and Lutronia, the last to forge the bridge slipped and fell—desperately clutching a sharp rock, saving her from a deadly fall. I rushed to help her up to safety. We finally both made it to the top of the monolith, greeted happily by Elizabeth and my sisters. Rock began to fall from the walls around us.

"We're out of time," I shouted. "Elizabeth, show them the way out. Don't wait for me." She protested, but I made sure she and the girls left. Samo refused to leave my side.

I looked out over the cavern. I saw Elizabeth and the others across the way, making steps to the tunnel to the outside world. I turned to the altar, and approached it.

The Sun Stone was magnificent. It was hard to believe that I was part of the story contained in its runes. The ground beneath me swayed and a big rock landed hard right next to me, barely missing my head.

Amid the rising dust and crescendoing noise, I pulled the crystal from my clothing and fondled its warmth one last time. I don't know why, but I raised it above my head and plunged it down, sinking it deeply into the hole from which I had pulled it not too long ago. Immediately, I got a shock, and energy escaped from the crystal with a loud boom. I shielded my face from the heat but the force knocked me down.

I got up and scrambled to the stairs and bounded down, reaching the bottom in seconds. I looked up to see the stone bridge retreat crustily into the wall of the cavern, and the entrance to the tunnel collapse and fill with rock.

I made my way through the tunnel, and found everyone waiting for me.

"Hurry," they all screamed. The rumbling became unbearable and the tunnel creaked and roared with the sound of colliding rock.

Two more steps. I lept at them, and knocked them all down the slope. We rolled and rolled until we hit the savannah floor. Above us, the cave crumbled and the rumbling stopped. We were surrounded by complete silence. I crawled to Elizabeth's side and she raised her head, smiling. My sisters seemed to be all right and we embraced and gathered together for a moment of thankfulness. In these special first moments, I felt it impossible, but if anything had stayed with me over these past wonderful days was the absolute certainty that nothing is impossible. We might, someday, find our way back again. Or perhaps not. But I was sure we would all try.

Elizabeth called to me, "Come on, Alan. Move it. You know the way. I'm starting to get hungry!"

"Oh, Elizabeth. Can't you forget about food for just a few days?" I playfully kidded her.

The princesses laughed.

The adaptability of the human spirit is indescribable. What luck—lost with five absolute beauties in nowhere land, home of cannibals and hungry hyenas. And I without a gun. Alan, I thought to myself, five women depend on you, so don't panic. Don't think, just move! After three deep breaths I felt reassured.

The lay of the land became increasingly familiar. The promising horizon lay before us. The tall, green grass to the West meant water and food. More importantly, though, somewhere out there, not so far away, was a future waiting for all of us. We just had to let it be so.

"All right, my lovely ladies," I ordered, "get moving! We still have a long way to go!"

They all stopped and looked at me, unmistakably recognized the commanding tone in my voice. Rightly so, for we were now in my part of the country, my world.

I placed my hat on my head and lifted Samo up on my left shoulder—his favorite place to travel—and started down the slope.

They all followed, like the stars have always followed the sunset.

THE END

Elizabeth and I eventually settled in the cold, north lands of Russia. My sisters went their separate ways, each to a far-away land, and had families of their own. The last time I heard from any of them was several years ago. It was curious, probably just one more strange coincidence, but each settled at the far corner of the world, where a piece of the Sun Stone had been so long ago.

As for Elizabeth and I, we were blessed with one son. It wasn't until he was old enough to understand that we told him the story of Chandi. At first, he thought it was a fairy tale, and I must have told him the story a hundred times before he went to sleep. He told me that when he grows up, he, too, will go to Africa—to find his own Kingdom of Chandi.

Perhaps, someday, he will.

Because as it was written...

But from his seed another king shall emerge, this one shall
Return to the Golden Land to establish a new kingdom,
the new Chandi.
He shall bequeath to the land Four Treasures
that will cause the
New kingdom to be mighty and prosperous.

The first shall be a great wall to stop the sacred waters
For the benefit of the land and all who live in it.
The waters that nurture the earth will be captive
And quench the thirst for all living things.

The second shall be the establishment of wildlife long missing,
To again walk the earth and live together in natural bliss.
The lion and the kudu shall coexist as brothers and
The birds of the sky find refuge in the trees.

Mighty and great shall be the new land,
For the Third Treasure opens the new Chandi
To the world, to cause it to share its bounty and
Prosperity with those in the far reaches of the world.
Lastly, the progeny of the last Sun King
Shall return to the new Kingdom from the four corners
Of the world, to live and work ever diligently, to build a great
Palace in the new Kingdom as a beacon to the world.

So it will be!

In 1992, in the heart of South Africa, a magical place called The Palace of The Lost City came to be, due to the intrinsic desire of a powerful man and with the help of many people that came from the four corners of the world to help him build his dream. Curiously this man was also known in Africa as...

The Sun King

To Sol Kerzner, the dream creator.

ACKNOWLEDGEMENTS

from the Author Eduardo A. Robles

The core of these stories only existed in the minds of the people who designed the Lost City.

Designers as Jerry Allison, Henry Conversano, Thanu Boonyawatana, Bernardo Munoz and myself, created the basis of some of these stories as inspirational tools in the design process during the construction of The Palace of the Lost City in South Africa.

When the project came to completion in December 1992, all these stories and legends that were still vague in format began to materialize in my mind as a fictional novel and six months later I got into the task to put my thoughts in writing.

With lots of fun and between a world of fantasies of heroes and sorcerers, valleys and kings, I was able to complete this book with the help of my sister Blanca Rosa and illustrations by my friend and partner, Thanu Boonyawatana.

All these fantastic stories are as real as you want to believe they are.

Who knows, it is very possible that maybe when you are reading some of these stories you might find yourself in the middle of The Palace's beautiful chambers or extensive gardens or maybe in some magical way you'll be part of the stories that I'm telling you.

It is my belief that The Palace and the Lost City will always exist as a magical place in Africa because it is part of an unfinished adventurous world where fantasy and reality coexist.

THE PALACE OF THE LOST CITY